Strategic Value

Value analysis as a business weapon

Strategic Value

Value analysis as a business weapon

Richard Stewart

HarperCollins*Publishers*

HarperCollins*Publishers*

First published in Australia in 2012
by HarperCollins*Publishers* Australia Pty Limited
ABN 36 009 913 517
harpercollins.com.au

HarperCollins*Publishers*
Level 13, 201 Elizabeth Street, Sydney NSW 2000
31 View Road, Glenfield, Auckland 0627, New Zealand
A 53, Sector 57, Noida, UP, India
77–85 Fulham Palace Road, London W6 8JB, United Kingdom
2 Bloor Street East, 20th floor, Toronto, Ontario M4W 1A8, Canada
10 East 53rd Street, New York NY 10022, USA

ISBN 978 0 7322 9559 2

Front and back cover image ©iStockPhoto/Ubbo
Editorial and production by Red Hill Publishing redhillpublishing.com
Cover designed by www.covecreative.com.au

Contents

Introduction

On Monday, 15 September 2008, US Treasury Secretary Henry Paulson made an urgent address to the White House. In a masterful piece of understatement, Paulson began: 'Well, as you know, we're working through a difficult period in our financial markets right now ...' Paulson was, of course, referring to the events of earlier that day, when the firm Lehman Brothers — one of the largest US investment banks at the time — filed for Chapter 11 bankruptcy protection.

The Treasury Secretary continued his speech by warning that future uncertainty was probable and that, most likely, there would be 'rough spots' ahead.

If, by rough spots, Paulson meant the single greatest financial crisis since The Great Depression of the 1930s, he was right.

By filing for bankruptcy in September 2008, Lehman Brothers earned the dubious accolade of the largest bankruptcy in US history. Moreover, this landmark case ushered in an era of volatility, uncertainty and risk never before seen in financial markets.

The collapse of Lehmans saw the world sail headlong into the rough waters of the Global Financial Crisis (GFC). 'Sailing' is a particularly apt way of thinking about it. When I sat down to write a book about strategic valuation, I found I was constantly reminded of sailing because the two areas are strikingly similar. There's an art to valuation just as there's an art to sailing; both require skill and strategy; both, when carried out successfully, will see you pull ahead of the competition to achieve tangible results; and both require you to read your surrounding environment and make decisions based on your situation.

However, sailing wasn't the only analogy that rose to the surface when I was writing this book. It just so happens that some of my favourite pastimes — having a punt and, in particular, playing poker — apply just as much to business valuation. What's more, all three of these activities are arguably quite Australian indulgences, given that so many of us live near the coast and just as many of us are partial to a flutter. By using analogies that so many readers can relate to, I hope to add to your understanding of the valuation discipline.

So how do sailing, gambling and playing poker relate to business valuation? Simple. All three endeavours require participants to:

i)   understand what's at stake and understand the risk associated with that stake

ii)   understand the strategy with which you might improve your position.

Both of these aspects are covered extensively in this book.

Reading the conditions

Any sailor worth their salt knows to check the weather conditions before dragging the boat out. So what are conditions currently like in Australia? What effect did the GFC have on our financial environment? Is it worth getting our feet wet?

The GFC saw markets get battered, insecurity surface and consumer confidence sink without a trace. It was the perfect storm.

But — and this is key — while undeniably brutal, the GFC inflicted only limited damage on local markets. In fact, some industries and some individuals have weathered it remarkably well. As with any change in conditions, the GFC has brought opportunities, not just risks, and it's these opportunities that we have to seize in order to get the most out of the post-GFC market.

First, let's recap on the recent history of the market.

Figure 1: Australian and World Share Price Indices[1]

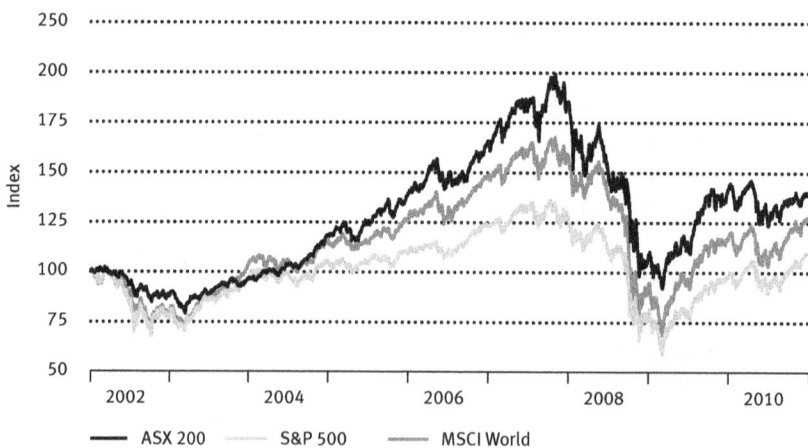

Note: 31 December 2011 = 100 Source: Bloomberg

Australian businesses responded swiftly to the economic downturn by cutting production and running down inventories, and this was reflected in share prices (see figure 1). According to Treasury, Australian businesses ran down their stocks by $3.4 billion (in real terms) in the December quarter 2008[2], the largest fall on record.

There was also a marked shift towards impairments (downward revaluation of assets) during the crisis. The IMF estimated this trend was worth US$4,400 billion by the end of the 2008 financial year alone[3] and Australia was no exception to the rule. A PwC Australia study[4] found that in FY08, 28 out of 197 sampled companies (or 14 per cent) reported a write-down of goodwill, and 22 companies (11 per cent) reported a write-down of other identifiable intangibles. These write-downs were worth $2.1 billion and $0.4 billion respectively. The Australian Securities and Investments Commission (ASIC) found write-downs to be 5 per cent of the total value of indefinite lived intangible assets and goodwill for the 12 months to 31 December 2009. For the 12 months to 30 June 2009, write-downs were 11 per cent.[5] There's no mistaking that the GFC made serious waves.

The extent of these waves can be seen in the VIX graph for the period 1999–2009 (see figure 2). This graph is a measure of implied volatility and shows the level of uncertainty in the market. As you can see, it wasn't just value that shifted during recent years; so too did people's uncertainty about value. In fact, the level of uncertainty around the GFC was the most significant in at least 10 years. Confidence, it seems, has been at a premium of late.

Figure 2: Implied Volatility (VIX) graph 1999–2009

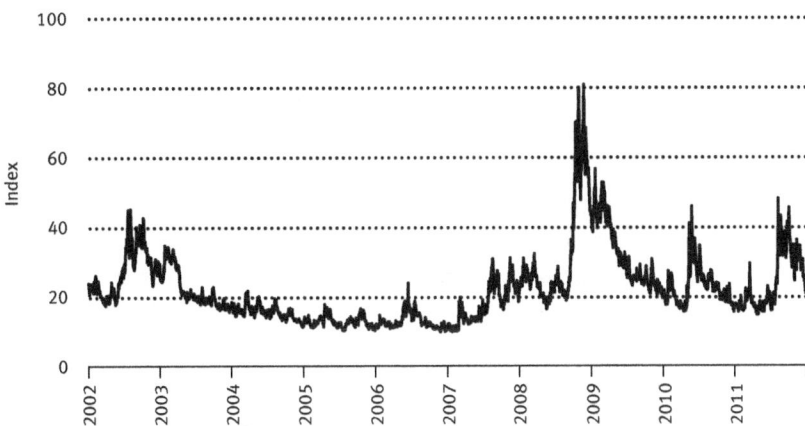

Source: Bloomberg

You won't be surprised to learn, then, that when 2009 rolled around more capital was being raised by the big end of town than at any time in recent memory.

2010 was a year characterised by takeovers. *The Australian*'s Rebecca Urban reported in August 2010: 'While the volume of corporate activity slowed about 20 per cent locally during the first half of 2010, several Australian companies have been among some of the largest takeover deals announced worldwide'.[6] Because so many companies during this period were trading at substantial discounts, and with less capital behind them, they were leaving themselves exposed to takeover bids. Some rejected advances (in many cases at a cost to their reputation); some acquiesced, rather than risk a long (and often futile) fight; and some toughed it out for a better deal. Whatever the outcome, the increased merger and acquisition activity only added to the shakiness of the market.

Sailing towards a brighter future

Post-GFC many investors are, understandably, still very nervous about the prevailing economic climate. Some investors blame market value accounting (which can increase the volatility of reported earnings) for their nerves, and directors from all sectors have been feeling jittery about the carrying value of assets purchased in the run-up to the collapse.

Despite the recent upturn, there are still a lot of nervous people out there.

Of course, value is all about expectations of the future. From an economist's viewpoint, valuation compares a certain cash flow now (that is, the price) with an uncertain stream of cash flows in the future. The major challenge associated with valuation lies in understanding these future cash flows. Given that the future can change so very rapidly, as it did on that single day in September 2008, you'd better be ready to adjust your expectations accordingly. It's no longer good enough to think of value as a certainty.

That's not to say another storm like the GFC is a certainty. But if you've weathered the storm of the past few years (or even if you capsized along the way) there are some important lessons to be learned from riding the rough seas of global economic uncertainty. Most importantly, we all need to be aware of the risks and the opportunities around value.

This is why I've written this book now. With enough water under the bridge since the crisis first shook financial markets (and with the luxury of a fairly even keel here in Australia, when compared to other markets around the world), it's vital we recognise what we did wrong to avoid making the same mistakes again, as well as what we can do right, to make the most of the prevailing economic conditions.

Valuation fluctuations

One common mistake when it comes to valuation is to think of value as a fixed number. This can be seen day in and day out, in boardrooms right across the country. It's easy to think that because value is set at X amount today that it will be roughly the same tomorrow. This 'gut feel' or approximate approach to value can be difficult to shake. The reality, however, is that — depending on the asset — its value could be radically different in the future. A case in point, and where fluctuations can be particularly acute, is derivatives. Because of the impact of leverage, $1 million today might easily be minus $1 million tomorrow.

Of course, this means that our 'gut feel' way of thinking about value (that is, conceiving of value as roughly constant) doesn't translate to the balance sheet. For instance, in October 2010 *The Australian Financial Review*[7] reported that the Reserve Bank of Australia (RBA) suffered a record valuation loss of $3.8 billion off the back of the strength of the Aussie dollar in mid-2010. The notion that the value of Australia's central bank can be so capricious may sound surprising but, of course, the RBA is custodian of the nation's official foreign reserves so it is at the mercy of currency fluctuations.

Because assets don't behave as we think they should — they don't remain stagnant and are susceptible to upward or downward movements — we can't ignore our valuation instruments and just fly by the seat of our pants.

Consider the phenomenon of Pilot Induced Oscillation (PIO). PIO occurs when pilots become so disoriented that they disbelieve the instruments in the dashboard and instead try to reorient themselves according to where they think the ground should be. More often than not, this particularly cruel affliction causes pilots to fly themselves into the ground, despite what their instruments are screaming at them.

By ignoring all the signs, we risk losing out in the valuation stakes. Or, at least, not winning as much as we could. Our assets might not behave as instinct would suggest so we have to rely on more rigorous analyses of value. Part of this includes recognising that value is both variable and relative. Just as in a race it doesn't matter how fast you're going if someone else is going faster, if your assets are going up less quickly than your competitors', there's still room for you to add value. Part III of this book shows how you can use all the valuation instruments you have to hand to make sure you're doing just that.

Who should read this book?

Among the flotsam and jetsam washed up in the wake of the global financial crisis there is one key lesson for us all: value now lies at the core of any organisation. Given the volatility and the uncertainty of our post-GFC world, it's more important than ever to understand value and to be able to assess value regardless of your role within a company. We can no longer afford to leave value up to someone else.

So, with this in mind, who should read this book?

→ those involved in valuation for a living
→ CFOs and senior financial executives
→ heads of strategy

$\rightarrow$ investors (especially corporate portfolio managers, like private equity fund managers)

$\rightarrow$ all other organisational members.

But just because we all need a working understanding of value doesn't mean we must all be experts on every aspect of valuation. Each reader should read this book in a different way. As a starting point, the following matrix highlights which sections will be most useful, depending on your role within an organisation.

Who should read what?

	Part I: How much is my business worth?	Part II: How do I assess risks to value?	Part III: How can I increase value?	Key Takeaways
Valuers	✓	✓		✓
CFOs	✓		✓	✓
Heads of strategy		✓	✓	✓
Fund managers		✓	✓	✓
Other investors		✓	✓	✓
Other organisational members			✓	✓

At least one section applies directly to every member of any organisation. This book is not a technical treatise but a commonsense review, with examples that illustrate key concepts to make it accessible and memorable, no matter what your role or capacity in a company may be.

How should I read this book?

This book is divided into three sections.

The first section, 'How much is my business worth?', provides a general understanding of how valuations are conducted. It looks at valuation for a variety of purposes (including valuation for investment decision making and for regulatory obligations), as well as in special industry circumstances. In sailing terms, the initial chapters of this book run you through all the essentials, from how to hoist the sails to when to trim the jib, making for plain sailing.

Part II is where you venture into uncharted waters. Titled 'How do I assess risks to value?', this section guides you through what to do when things go wrong. Because things do go wrong and, as the GFC showed us, volatility is the new reality. This second section acknowledges that value is an uncertain issue by definition, because it's all about predicting the future. Just as any sailor practises 'person overboard' drills, it's important to understand the variety of ways the future might unfold and to plan for each of these different scenarios. Part II equips you with four ways of analysing risk because when the stakes are high and the risks are real, knowledge is power.

The final section of this book delivers five ways in which a senior executive can improve the value of their business. By revealing real opportunities to add value, and exposing 'pump and dump' imitations, Part III explains that the role of management and boards is to increase value, and then shows you how this can be done.

Graphically, the book looks like this:

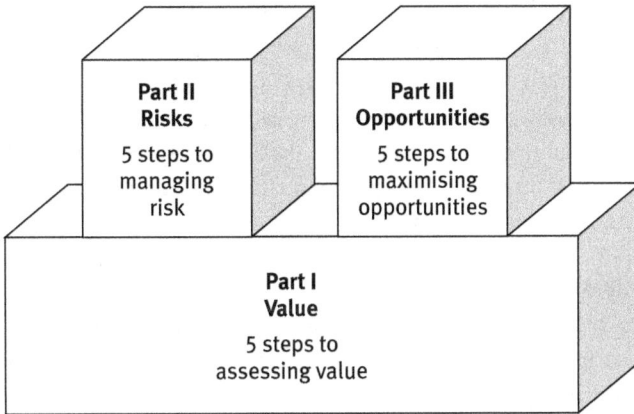

```
Part II                    Part III
Risks                      Opportunities

5 steps to                 5 steps to
managing                   maximising
risk                       opportunities

          Part I
          Value

        5 steps to
     assessing value
```

The three topics of value, risks and opportunities are indivisible, so each of the three sections of this book are integral to the whole. It's essential we understand all three blocks in order to manage value effectively.

The importance of strategy

If the GFC was the stock market impact of the downturn, then the write-downs of FY08–09 represent the accounting impact. Given we're talking about impairments to the tune of US$4,400 billion globally for FY08 alone, it's pertinent to ask: Did the business world get things wrong?

The answer is simply that, until now, we've thought about value too narrowly. This is why this book is structured in three sections. First, we need to get the basics of valuation right. Next, it's imperative we understand the risks involved and anticipate what might go wrong, in order to cope with a (likely) volatile future. Only then can we embark on more sophisticated strategising around value.

To understand the importance of strategy, take the story of 'Mr America's Cup', Dennis Conner, and his shock loss to Alan Bond's *Australia II* in the world's greatest sailing race back in 1983. This was a loss based in part on second-rate strategy.

When Dennis Conner and his 12-metre yacht *Liberty* faced *Australia II* in the America's Cup off Rhode Island all those years ago, his game plan simply wasn't up to the tactics employed by the Australians.

In what would have been the final leg, *Liberty* took the lead and was in front of *Australia II* by over a minute when Australian skipper, John Bertrand, tacked away and caught a shift. Here, *Liberty* should have mirrored their competitor's move from in front so that *Australia II* could never overtake. But he didn't. By playing the external conditions to their advantage, *Australia II* was able to steal and maintain the lead.

When *Australia II* won, they ended the New York Yachting Club's 132-year hold on the America's Cup and, with it, the longest winning streak in sporting history. This was all down to a superior strategy — and some pretty good technology too; remember Ben Lexcen's winged keel? Same conditions, same opportunities: just a more advanced plan of attack.

Business valuation works in exactly the same way. By employing a more advanced plan of attack, by being strategic in your approach, suddenly value becomes your greatest weapon.

KEY TAKEAWAYS

→ Post-GFC, we're operating in an era of volatility and risk the like of which has never before been seen in financial markets, so it's no longer good enough to think of value as a certainty.

→ However, these conditions bring not just risk but also opportunities to those who understand business valuation.

→ With this in mind, it's more important than ever to understand value and to be able to assess value regardless of your role within a company.

FURTHER READING

Ross Garnaut, *The Great Crash of 2008*, Melbourne University Press, Melbourne, 2009.
John Bertrand, *Born to Win*, Bantam Publishing, Sydney, 1985.

Part I

How much is my business worth?

Chapter 1

Setting the course: price versus value

A cynic is a man who knows the price of everything but the value of nothing. — Oscar Wilde

As a sailor, every time you set foot on an unfamiliar boat you need to learn the ropes. Each boat is different, so it's important to run through the basics to avoid running into trouble later on. For instance, do you know where the life jackets are kept? What about the first aid kit? Have you checked how the marine radio works? How about the GPS? Then, let's not forget the most important question for every good sailor: Where can I find a cold beer? In just the same way, before we learn how to be strategic about value, we need to understand the fundamentals.

Price versus value

A key point in understanding value is to recognise that price and value are not necessarily the same. Value is what something is worth to you. Price is what it might be sold for in an open exchange. You know that hideous artwork your friends recently paid a fortune for? That's a good example of the difference between price and value. To your mind, that 'artwork' is not worth the canvas it's painted on yet they've just mortgaged the house to buy it. Clearly, the value you place on the painting and the price paid for the painting do not match.

In the marketplace, however, things are not so cut and dried. Usually, when we refer to value in the marketplace, we're relying on the conventional (and very specific) definition of value. This definition of market value is 'the price that would be negotiated in an open and unrestricted market between a knowledgeable, willing (but not anxious) buyer and a knowledgeable, willing (but not anxious) seller acting at arm's length.'[8] So value is generally understood to be the price negotiated.

Didn't we say value and price are not the same thing? Yet the definition provided by the Australian Taxation Office (ATO) uses the terms 'value' and 'price' interchangeably.

What the ATO is actually defining here is price or, more accurately, how you might go about estimating price. It's not a true, complete definition of value. So don't be swayed from our first lesson — value is separate from price.

Consider the real estate market. Just as in any other market, different buyers and different sellers have different views of value. If you and I are standing next to each other at an auction waiting to bid on the same townhouse, chances are that one of us values that house more than the other. I may have my eye on a similar property in the next suburb, in which I would just as happily live. You, on the other hand, might own the townhouse next door and have grand plans to demolish them both and rebuild. Clearly, this house is worth more to you than it is to me and our different views on value will be reflected in the price we're prepared to pay. It's these different views of value that make a market. If everyone had the same view of value, no one would buy or sell anything because there's nothing to be gained by the trade. Within a market, value necessarily differs between players, even though price is generally agreed upon.

The best illustration of this is in mergers and acquisitions, shown by this figure.

Figure 3: Valuation in practice[9]

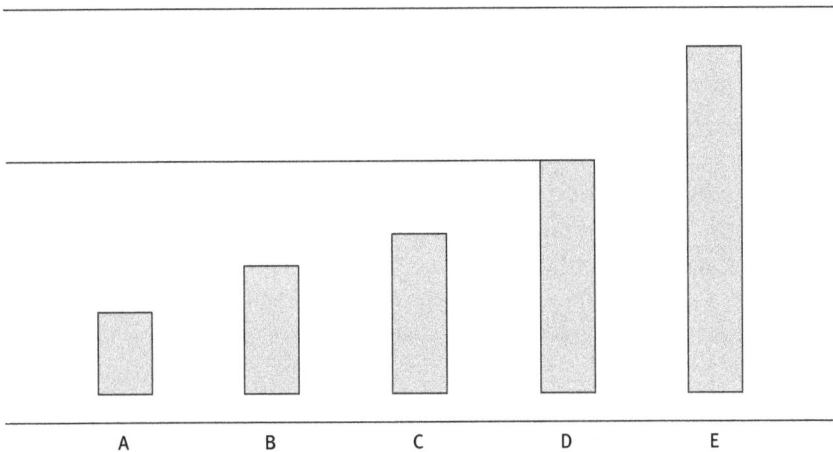

Here A is the seller of an asset (and column A is the value to this seller). B, C, D and E are all bidders and all have very different views of value (shown by the varying heights of columns B, C, D and E).

A shouldn't sell their asset for the amount they value it at (i.e. column A) because everyone else has a higher view of its value. There's money to be made here.

If this graph represented the house auction we talked about, the person that's going to walk away with the deeds to the property is probably E because E values the house the most.

But if E is sensible, they will never pay much more than what the property is worth to the next highest bidder — that is, D — because that's all E needs to spend to win the auction. So, assuming a sensible market, the price paid will be at or near point D. Compare this single price point to value, which is all over the place, depending on who you ask about the asset's worth.

> ⟪⟪ A key point for understanding value is to recognise
> that price and value are not necessarily the
> same. ⟫⟫

What often happens in mergers and acquisitions is that price and value are confused. Say C pays the going price for this asset (which is at point D, remember). This is more than the asset is worth to C, so C loses the difference between column D and column C. By confusing the concepts of value and price, people such as C can make bad decisions.

Then there are the games taking place within the market. If I were A, I would be talking up the asset to all the players involved. Say the issue was synergies and this was a corporate takeover; A should try to convince B, C and D that the synergies are just as big as E thinks they are and so they should reassess their estimates of value (and therefore what they're prepared to pay) upwards. This can be harder than it looks; in fact, some people maintain that humans just aren't wired for this type of value-oriented thinking.[10]

Perception is everything

As the introduction outlined, value is about expectations of the future. So the only thing certain about the future, and therefore value, is that it's not certain; it's all about perceptions. It follows that if you can change people's perceptions about value then you have the ability to shift the price, and that is where things start to get interesting.

> ⟪⟪ It follows that if you can change people's perceptions
> about value then you have the ability to shift the price,
> and that is where things start to get interesting. ⟫⟫

A great example is the AGL Energy takeover of oil and gas explorer, Mosaic Oil NL. This is a case I was involved in: PwC, where I'm a partner, provided the independent expert's report to Mosaic. In the report, PwC recommended that Mosaic accept AGL's offer, and assessed the fair market value of Mosaic shares to be between $0.128 and $0.197. This price doesn't mean much until you consider the value of Mosaic to AGL. You see, AGL was looking to buy out Mosaic as part of a bigger strategy to own Mosaic's depleted oil field in central Queensland. The field in question was spent, so was of little obvious value to anyone. Except AGL. AGL just so happened to need a gas storage plant in Central Queensland and the empty Mosaic field fit the bill perfectly. Moreover, while the empty field was tremendously valuable to the acquirer, it was basically worthless to everyone else, so AGL was able to pay a minimal (but fair) price.

AGL paid somewhere down around A on our earlier graph, because there was no competition from B, C or D to push the price up. So the price paid by AGL was significantly below the value they placed on the asset; AGL got a bargain when compared to the value they obtained.

Price variations

Another difference between price and value is the fluctuations that price is subject to. There's a whole range of reasons why prices are different in different circumstances yet intrinsic value remains relatively the same.

Say you own shares in Qantas. More specifically, say you own one share. If I were to tell you that you can't currently sell that share, it would be worth less than if you could go out and sell it tomorrow. Why? Because there's a risk it might depreciate between now and the time you're permitted to sell it. This is even worse if other Qantas shares are privately held. You might have one share, but say someone else owns all the other shares: your lonely share is barely worth anything at all because you could be marginalised at any minute. (But not egregiously so, as there are laws around that).

Or imagine you had designs on buying all of Qantas, not just one share. In this case, you might be willing to pay much more per share because it would award you control of the company. Or perhaps there's an opportunity for Qantas to share travel routes with British Airways. Again, suddenly you'd be prepared to fork out a little more for a cut of that scenario. In short, value depends on circumstance.

> There is a whole raft of reasons why the circumstances surrounding an asset alter the price you'd be willing to pay, even though they don't change the fundamental value of the asset to you.

There is a whole raft of reasons why the circumstances surrounding an asset alter the price you'd be willing to pay, even though they don't change the fundamental value of the asset to you. To understand more about why price varies in different circumstances, see the figure here.[11]

Figure 4: Valuation in practice

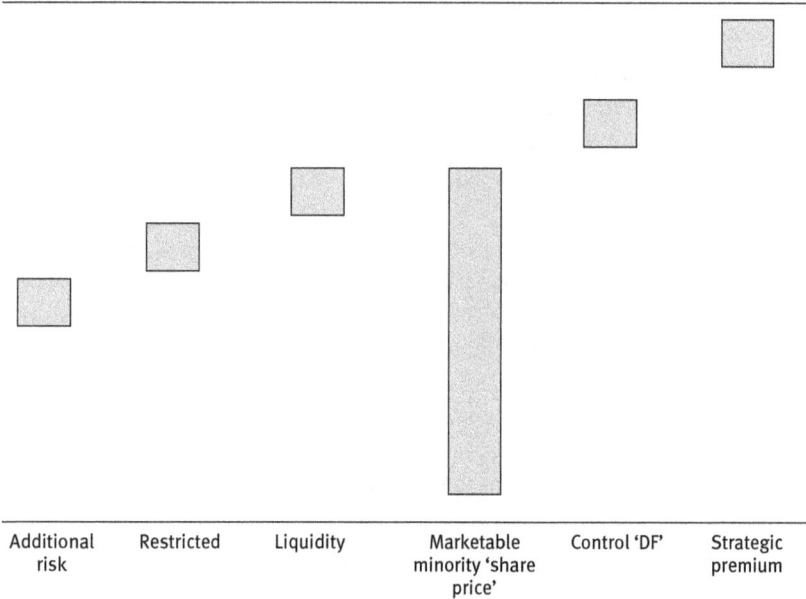

| Additional risk | Restricted | Liquidity | Marketable minority 'share price' | Control 'DF' | Strategic premium |

Consider the normal share price of Qantas as the middle (tall) bar in this graph. A financial buyer would need to pay a premium just to acquire control. A strategic buyer, say another airline, would likely be able (and would be required) to pay a further premium — a strategic premium — because of the synergies they may be able to access.

On the other hand, a share that is difficult or time-consuming to sell will generally be valued at a discount to the normal minority share value. This discount is usually even larger if you are prevented from selling the share (i.e. it is restricted). Finally, there may be other conditions that add risk to particular shares (say vesting conditions to the share, which don't entitle you to own the share unless some performance condition is satisfied) that further depress value in those circumstances.

> This book looks at value in terms of how you can assess it and how you can add it.

Having determined the difference between price and value, the remainder of this book focuses on value. However, this book is not based on the traditional definition of value discussed above — i.e. the price that would be negotiated in an open and unrestricted market between a knowledgeable, willing (but not anxious) buyer and a knowledgeable, willing (but not anxious) seller acting at arm's length. Because as we now know, all this definition is talking about is price. Plus there are already any number of books out there doing that.

> ❝ Why are you doing a valuation? What do you hope to achieve? Are you planning to sell the business? Is it to settle a dispute? ❞

Instead, this book sets a different course and looks at value in terms of how you can assess it and how you can add it.

Steps to a valuation

If you're going to work out value, how do you go about it?

The first important step is to ascertain your purpose. Why are you doing a valuation? What do you hope to achieve? Are you planning to sell the business? Is it to settle a dispute? Perhaps you need to determine the impact on value of certain proposed changes to the business? Or maybe you just need a number for some form of negotiation?

The reason for your valuation will affect the steps you take to your valuation, because different circumstances will require a different approach. Certainly, different circumstances will require you to present your findings quite differently. If you're considering how to improve the business, the valuation you present to the board will be vastly different from the sort of valuation report a legal dispute would require. For examples of some of the various contexts for valuation, see figure 5: Business valuation in context.[12]

Figure 5: Business valuation in context

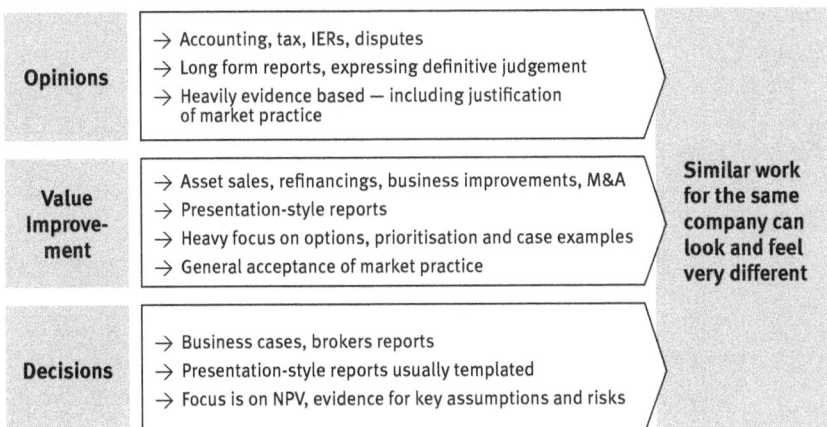

Opinions	→ Accounting, tax, IERs, disputes → Long form reports, expressing definitive judgement → Heavily evidence based — including justification of market practice	
Value Improve-ment	→ Asset sales, refinancings, business improvements, M&A → Presentation-style reports → Heavy focus on options, prioritisation and case examples → General acceptance of market practice	**Similar work for the same company can look and feel very different**
Decisions	→ Business cases, brokers reports → Presentation-style reports usually templated → Focus is on NPV, evidence for key assumptions and risks	

Yet despite the differing circumstances, the basic underlying valuation analysis would be quite similar in each case. So let's take a closer look at this valuation analysis.

Setting the course

The remainder of Part I is set out like this:

Chapter 2		Chapters 3, 4 and 5
Strategic analysis	**Financial analysis**	**Perform valuation**
Industry	Historic	Technique
Competitive position	Forecasts	Parameters
Plans	Benchmarks	Cross check

'Strategic Analysis' kicks off in Chapter 2. This explains how to carry out a strategic analysis and covers all aspects of strategy, such as industry, competitive position (including your competition, marketing and cost structure) and future plans.

Chapter 2 also looks at your 'Financial Analysis'. This is where you run the numbers, interpreting historical data, future forecasts and external and internal benchmarks.

Finally, in Chapters 3, 4 and 5 you can get your hands dirty and do a valuation yourself. This covers the three valuation techniques available to you:

i)   income-based valuation
ii)   market-based valuation
iii) asset- or cost-based valuation.

These three chapters look at valuation in the context of several specific industries, too.

Here, you are also introduced to the idea of triangulating. That is, if you put value at $2 million and the market indicates it's more like half that figure, it's probable that you've done something wrong.

KEY TAKEAWAYS

→ A key point for understanding value is to recognise that price and value are not necessarily the same.

→ While you stand to lose a lot by confusing the two, there's also much to be gained by recognising the difference between price and value.

→ Divergent views on value are reconciled by the market to a single price.

→ Value depends not only on intrinsic value but also on circumstance.

→ Value is inherently uncertain, because it is all about the future.

→   Valuations often look different because of context. In reality they depend on the same fundamentals.

FURTHER READING

William Poundstone, *Priceless: The Myth of Fair Value (and how to take advantage of it)*, Hill & Wang, New York, 2010.

Wayne Lonergan, *The Valuation of Businesses, Shares and Other Equity*, Allen and Unwin, Crows Nest, 2003.

Paul Milgrom, *Putting Auction Theory to Work*, Cambridge University Press, Cambridge, 2004.

Charles W. Smith, *Auctions: The Social Constructions of Value*, The Free Press, London, 1990.

Chapter 2

Conducting a strategic and financial analysis

However beautiful the strategy, you should occasionally look at the results. — Sir Winston Churchill

In Lewis Carroll's timeless classic, *Alice's Adventures in Wonderland,* Alice asked the Cheshire Cat: 'Would you tell me, please, which way I ought to go from here?' The response? 'That depends a good deal on where you want to get to,' said the Cat. 'I don't much care where,' said Alice. 'Then it doesn't matter which way you go,' said the Cat.

Strategy and results, it seems, are inextricably linked. If you don't know what results you're aiming for it's nearly impossible to work out the best way to achieve them. Likewise, if you never plan how you're going to meet your goals, it's unlikely you'll ever do so.

When determining how much your business is worth you need to conduct a strategic and a financial analysis. A strategic analysis will allow you to look at your business in context — that is, where you sit in terms of your industry and the broader economy — as well as your current plans to address the context. A financial analysis, on the other hand, will show you the results of those plans.

Looking at results without strategy only tells half the story, and concentrating on strategy but not results won't even give you that much. It seems, when it comes to valuation, the Cheshire Cat was on the money.

Nine basic questions
When approaching valuation, and before conducting a strategic or financial analysis, there are nine basic questions you should always ask:

    i)   What is the history of the business?

ii) What logical divisions are there within the business (e.g. products, customers, operations, functions)?

iii) Who are its customers and suppliers? What are the terms of trade like?

iv) Who are the major competitors?

v) How is business conducted and how does the business compete in order to make money (i.e. what are the critical assets of the business)?

vi) What are the emerging trends/outlook within the business?

vii) How is ownership of the business organised?

viii) Have there been any one-off events that have impacted (or will impact) the business?

ix) What are the major risks in the business?

Strategic analysis

When these questions are answered it's time to move on to the strategic analysis. Whenever I have half a chance, nothing gives me more pleasure than to take the boat out on Sydney's Middle Harbour. This doesn't happen as often as I'd like but I manage to stretch the process out by spending the days preceding checking the Bureau of Meteorology website, checking the condition of the boat and checking over our sailing plan. In just the same way, in order to ascertain the strategic position of your business you must analyse the external environment, the condition of the business itself and your plans for the future.

Traditionally, a strategic analysis is conducted top-down and covers the economy, the industry and the company's specific plans. Let's consider each of these.

The economy

Looking at the general economic conditions of your operating environment is a very basic but not insignificant consideration. The economy in which your company and the broader industry reside is a good starting point for your valuation. In fact, the general conditions of demand should be the very first thing you look at and this should happen before your strategy is even at blueprint stage.

The industry

While the state of the overall economy is fundamental, this is where your strategic analysis starts in earnest. The first real unit of analysis when looking at a business is the industry in which it sits.

Assessing your industry means looking at three components:

i) the source of demand for your product

ii) how the competition is organised and its basis

iii) how well you compete within the industry.

Let's consider each of those elements in more detail.

Source of demand for your product

In principle, you can work out where demand for your product is coming from by looking at the nature of your product, who it's demanded by and what's happening with demand more broadly. For instance, demand can vary depending on the type of product you're looking at. Is it an intermediate product that depends on demand for other products? Is it a final or end-user product?

To illustrate, let's take one of the most successful products of the 2010s — Apple's iPad. How would you go about estimating demand for an iPad? There are several different dimensions to consider here.

Firstly, how many people would find the iPad a valuable tool? Let's start with the entire population of Australia and exclude, for argument's sake, those below five years of age and those over 65 years of age, as they're less likely to be iPad users. That means, of the 20 million people living in Australia, roughly 10 million fall into our residual category of potential iPad customers.

Then you need to consider that cost is going to rule out certain socio-economic groups, and even certain professions. Of the 10-million-strong market we just identified, let's say only 30 per cent of people can afford an iPad, so we're down to three million potential customers already.

Let's not forget that most of those three million own a digital device already. If we estimate that those devices are replaced every three years, our average market is suddenly one million units per annum — and that's only the available market. (According to a report in the *The Australian* on 19 October 2010, the iPad did quite well in this context, selling 250,000 units in its first six months.)

Next we must ask: What are the potential shares of that available market? That is, how much of that market can we reasonably expect to obtain? What are the competing technologies available to customers? How much of the market do they take up? There are Kindle, Kobo and Sony eReaders for a start, so what sort of market share can iPad reasonably expect? Work that out and you've estimated your demand.

Sounds simple, doesn't it? The good news is that it is, provided you do your homework and calculate accordingly. However, you'd be surprised how often people put business plans together that demonstrate the potential for massive growth but growth that can't be supported by the kind of back-of-the-envelope calculations we've just done for Apple's iPad. It's surprising, when you start thinking realistically about demand, just how quickly you reveal the source of improbability in some growth forecasts.

If you want to explore the concept of demand further, private equiteer Chris Golis provides a very simple but very effective analysis of the subject in his book *Enterprise and Venture Capital: A Business Builder's and Investor's Handbook* (see 'Further reading' for details). Golis provides perhaps the best analysis of how to estimate demand for a product that I've ever seen. But be warned: for something so simple, estimating demand is very rarely done effectively.

How the competition is organised and its basis

Once you've addressed demand for your product, it's important to consider the competition. The easiest way is by using Michael Porter's 'Five Forces' model for industry analysis and business strategy (see 'Further reading' for more details). Five Forces is the most common approach to understanding competition, for the simple reason that it is the best approach. This powerful yet elegant analysis looks at the bargaining power of each of the elements of your competitive environment. A strategic business manager gains an edge over any rivals by using this model to better understand the industry context in which they operate.

Graphically, Porter's Five Forces model looks like this:

Figure 6: Porter's 'Five Forces' model for industry analysis and business strategy

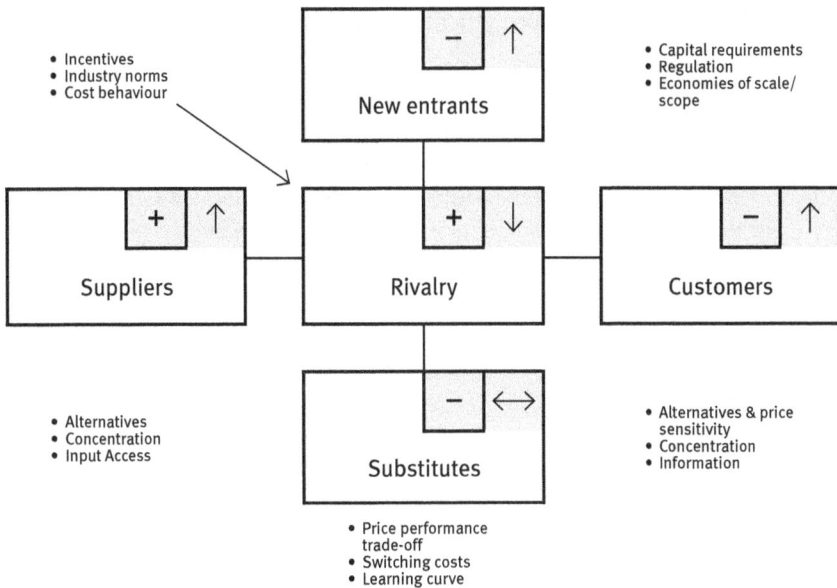

• Incentives
• Industry norms
• Cost behaviour

New entrants

• Capital requirements
• Regulation
• Economies of scale/ scope

Suppliers

Rivalry

Customers

• Alternatives
• Concentration
• Input Access

Substitutes

• Alternatives & price sensitivity
• Concentration
• Information

• Price performance trade-off
• Switching costs
• Learning curve

Note: + or − conveys a positive or negative effect on competitive position; the arrow indicates whether the force's influence is strengthening, weakening or staying the same.

Basically, the Five Forces analysis determines the competitive intensity and therefore attractiveness of a market. An attractive market offers the opportunity for overall industry profitability, whereas an unattractive industry sees these five forces working to drive down available economic profit.

Take Qantas as an example. By applying Porter's Five Forces model, your analysis of the airline industry would look like this.

1. Customers

Here, we consider the bargaining power of Qantas's customers. How many options do customers have? Can they go to many, many providers of airline services? Or are their choices quite limited? Internationally, airline customers can pick and choose but domestically, their bargaining power is more limited.

2. Suppliers

Who holds the cards when it comes to bargaining with suppliers? In Qantas's case this is Boeing and Airbus, and given there are only two aircraft suppliers to choose from (and many airlines doing the choosing), it's clear where the negotiating power lies here, even with the long lead times and large fixed costs of aircraft production.

The other type of supplier is the employees, and there's a more nuanced balance of power here. The airline industry has a highly unionised workforce but because there are only a few airlines, workers don't have as much choice in employer as they might enjoy in other industries.

3. Substitutes or competitors

When considering the threat of substitute products in any industry, it's useful to think about any switching costs involved and any price–performance trade-offs, as well as customer inclination to move. In the airline industry, complex frequent flyer initiatives do much to stave off this threat, but developments in video conferencing are starting to provide a viable substitute for air travel in certain circumstances.

4. New entrants or regulatory environment

What are the barriers to entry in the airline industry? Is the threat of new entrants high? Extensive government regulation of airlines, not to mention the exorbitant start-up costs, means new competitors are not common or are unlikely to survive. Just ask Compass Airlines.

5. Degree of rivalry between competitors

For many industries, the degree of competitive rivalry between players can be the deciding factor for industry competitiveness. Consider here things like industry concentration, cost structure and scale economics, industry growth and brand identity. Qantas enjoys strong brand identification — verging on the iconic — and limited competition locally. Meaning it's doing well in terms of the domestic industry, at least.

On balance, what these five forces determine is this: How good is the bargaining power of the company within its industry? This then determines how much profit the company is likely to make. (Profit, here, being economic profit; in other words, returns above the cost of capital.) In turn, this drives the so-called industry financial economics. Financial economics have two main components:

→ growth, which is essentially the growth in demand

→ the basis of competition, which determines the returns on capital (i.e. the returns derived within the industry).

Generally, the better bargaining position across the five forces, the more likely it is that returns will be above the cost of capital.

> Just because the industry is favourable, doesn't mean your profit is guaranteed; in an advantaged market it's still possible not to play the game well.

But there are exceptions. It is possible for a good company to thrive in a poor industry. Sticking with airlines, let's take USA's budget air carrier, Southwest Airlines, as an example. Southwest Airlines is bold, it's cheeky and it's done well. To give you a sense of Southwest's approach, its logo is a love heart; its common stock is traded under the symbol 'LUV' on the NYSE; and it regularly runs ads saying things like:

After lengthy deliberation at the highest executive levels, and extensive consultation with our legal department, we have arrived at an official corporate response to Northwest Airlines' claim to be number one in Customer Satisfaction. 'Liar, liar. Pants on fire.'[13]

Airlines the world over don't make much money but in the 1990s and early 2000s, Southwest was notably the exception to the rule. Although, as a recent industry analysis shows, it's hard to defy the gravity of your industry's economics forever. All the same, as one of the first budget air carriers to arrive on the scene, Southwest consistently makes quite good returns.

> ... it is feasible to have a situation where it's the company and not the broader industry that's underperforming.

Of course, it is feasible to have a situation where it's the company and not the broader industry that's underperforming. Just because the industry is favourable, doesn't mean your profit is guaranteed; in an advantaged market it's still entirely possible not to play the game well.

How well you compete within the industry

The third and final component when assessing industry is to consider how well you compete, or how well you're positioned, within your industry.

There are a number of great models available to help you work this out; again, I recommend Porter's method of analysis because he really is a guru in this area of strategic thought. Porter talks about two things that are important in determining where you sit in an industry: value chain and competitive advantage.

Value chain

When Porter refers to a value chain, he's talking about the set of activities between the primary resource and the end user of a product. For example, a value chain for the wine industry might look something like this:

Figure 7: Value chain analysis for the wine industry

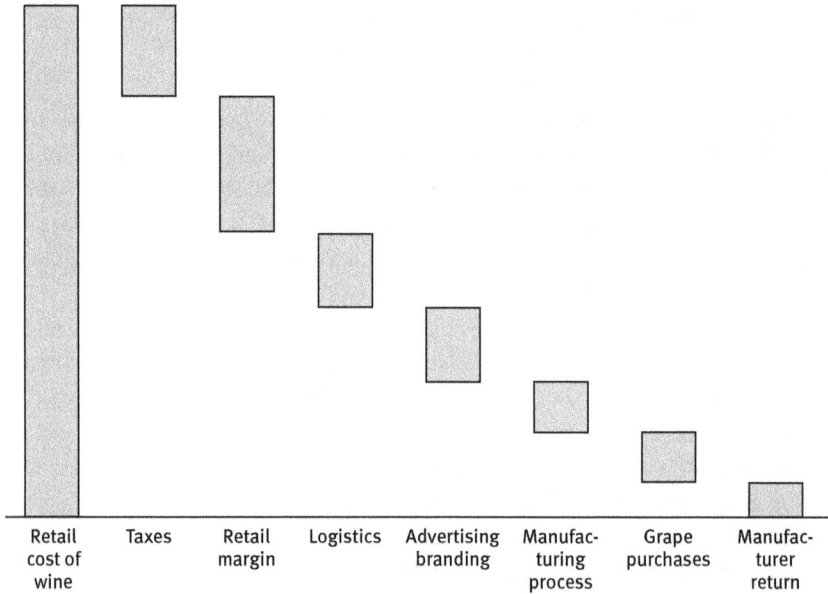

| Retail cost of wine | Taxes | Retail margin | Logistics | Advertising branding | Manufac- turing process | Grape purchases | Manufac- turer return |

> ⟪ Where you sit in the process can decide how significant your return is. ⟫

This set of activities awards the end product more added value than the sum of added values of all activities along the way. For instance, there are many steps involved between taking bauxite from the ground and turning it into an Audi: there's refinement, processing, assembly, design, and shipping involved. To say nothing of my favourite — the test-driving stage. Worth noting, however, is that each of these steps in the value chain provides very different returns, so where you sit in the process can decide how significant your return is. Porter talks about pinch points in the value chain, which are those points in the stream of activities where you can make more money than at any point in the rest of the value chain; say, because there's a skills shortage in your line of work.

> ⟪ Your advantage over your competitors directly affects your own return profile. ⟫

The next element of Porter's thinking, that of competitive advantage, allows you to understand how you compete well within your value chain. He also explains likely causes of this competitive advantage, so that you can leverage these factors for even better performance.

Figure 8: Porter's model of competitive advantage

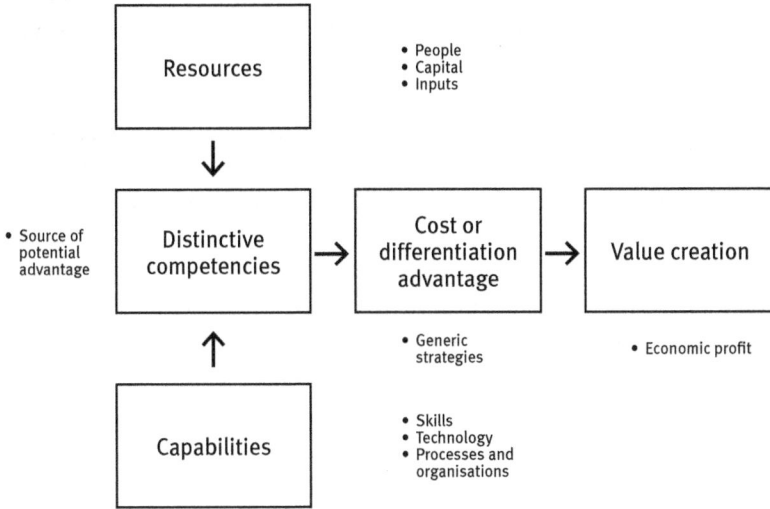

Your competitive advantage (with respect to your industry) drives what your own financial economics are, relative to your industry. This means your advantage over your competitors directly affects your own return profile, so if you compete well in your industry, you might enjoy a growth profile that is far above the industry's growth profile.

Before we leave the concept of competitive position it is worth noting that competitive positions can shift. Porter's models, while very good in many ways, are not dynamic models; they don't factor in change. They appreciate that your competitive situation exists relative to other players but they assume this situation is static. Under these assumptions you would make a move and no one else would respond to cancel this move out. As we well know, this is not reflected in reality.

A more realistic way of thinking about competition is to adopt the principles of John Forbes Nash Jr's game theory, made famous by the film *A Beautiful Mind*, starring Russell Crowe. The field of game theory, and in particular the idea of mutually assured destruction (MAD), was used extensively during the Cold War. MAD states that a full-scale use of nuclear weapons by two opposing sides would result in the eventual destruction of both sides, and that therefore (fortunately) such a conflict is unlikely — but that neither side, once armed, has any incentive to disarm.

You need to recognise that competitive positioning is dynamic and game theory provides a useful way to apply this to your industry. Your competitors are not going to stand around waiting for your next move any more than your customers are. In fact, the slogan 'innovate or perish' could just as easily read 'compete or perish' when it comes to industry positioning. Increasingly, companies across all sorts of industries are using game theory to try to understand how their competitive position might change because of the reactions of others.

Your company's plans

The discussion of sailing at the beginning of this chapter mentioned that a big part of pre-event preparation was race-day planning. Similarly, the third and final element to consider when conducting a strategic analysis is your own company's plans.

The strategic plans of your organisation are important because they provide a link between your competitive position now and your competitive position in the future. These plans should cover the key decisions that any company can make. From an operating point of view, these decisions are threefold.

1. Participation decisions

These decisions include:

→   Which markets do you want to operate in?
→   What products do you wish to sell?
→   Which customers are the best for you to be selling to?
→   What position on the value chain should you occupy?

2. Competitive decisions

Essentially, how do you compete? Here you should address four dimensions:

→   What offer are you putting to the market?
→   At what price?
→   What does your business model consist of?
→   What is your cost position?

Let's think about the competitive decisions of American jewellery company Tiffany & Co. (some of you will be on more intimate terms with the brand and know it as Tiffany's). Tiffany's offer is exceptionally exclusive jewellery and so their pricing is suitably expensive in order to match their offer. The Tiffany's business model is a very strong retail model. As I understand it you could say they don't manufacture the jewellery, they simply source it — so they are really a brand manager as opposed to a jewellery manufacturer. As for cost positioning? Cost is not a major factor for Tiffany's because this is a luxury product.

Everything is consistent in the Tiffany & Co. business model. The company's offer, pricing, cost positioning and business model are all in sync and their success reflects this.

On the other end of the scale, there are companies that have low price offers with a heavily integrated business model and poor cost positioning, and there can be no greater recipe for disaster.

3. Management structure

The third decision around operating is this: How might the management structure work? In light of the market you are operating in (decision one) and the way you compete (decision two), this third choice is essentially deciding on the best way for you to be organised. This decision is not as salient to value as the first two choices might be, but if management is aligned with the other two strategies, your organisation is more likely to be sustainable.

There are two further decisions to be made around planning that I should mention:

→ investments — these typically deal with the bets you plan to make around the other decisions

→ financing — these decisions deal with how you fund your bets.

This framework of strategic planning underpins the thinking throughout the rest of the book.

Financial analysis

These are the results Churchill was talking about in the quote at the beginning of this chapter and, as he so eloquently put it, you can't afford to underestimate their importance.

In terms of financial results, there are three components that are relevant:

i)   the historical performance of the business

ii)   the expected or forecast performance of the business

iii) the relative performance of the business, which is established through benchmarking.

There are five or six key things to look for when running the numbers on your business. These are known as value drivers and, as the name suggests, these drive the value of a product or service up (or down), increasing (or decreasing) value.

By way of example, the value drivers for an industrial company are:

→ What's the rate of sales growth?

→ What are the cash margins or EBITDA (Earnings Before Interest, Taxes, Depreciation and Amortisation) margins?

→ What are the capital requirements? (This is in terms of both fixed capital and working capital.)

→ What's the tax rate?

It is critical to understand each of these value drivers, as they form the basis for a whole series of further analyses (including time series or historical analysis and benchmarking, mentioned above).

Typically, you would pull up the last five to 10 years' worth of financial performance data and focus on the changes in value drivers from period to period. See the following table (over the page) for examples of the data typically gathered.

Figure 9: Historical and forecast financial analysis — Subject company and other companies in the same industry

Size and growth rates	Valuation (implied for subject)
→ sales → total assets → enterprise value (EV) and market cap	→ sales to EV → EBITDA and EBIT to EV → Equity value (Eq V) to NPAT and dividends → EV to ROIC → Eq V to Net book value → volatility, liquidity, takeover potential, overhang
Profitability → EBITDA margins → EBIT margins → NPAT margins → economic profit/residual income margins	**Credit** → debt to EV → debt to Equity (book) → debt to EBITDA → coverage → Interest (CF, EBIT[DA]) → FFO (CF, EBIT[DA]) → ratings
Return → ROIC → ROE → dividend yield and payout	
Capital consumption → stock, debtor and creditor days → fixed assets to sales	

However, there's one really important thing that needs to be done here and that's a Quality of Earnings Analysis (or normalisation). This is when you look at the performance of the business and remove any exceptional or misleading items. Those could be one-offs, or times where there have been changes in accounting policy or changes in estimates between accounting periods. Things like adjusting the way bad debt provisions are estimated. These one-offs don't change the business performance, merely the way you've estimated financial outcomes. So they shouldn't alter the underlying performance of the business.

When it comes to the history and the future of your financials, there are two critical points to remember. First, when looking at past performance, make sure you ask what's happened to returns on invested capital over a period of time. This is a sound measure of the financial economics discussed earlier.

Second, when it comes to forecasting, it's essential to factor in mean reversion. This is a simple idea — mean reversion is the tendency to revert back to the average — but it can have a significant effect. Interestingly, even biology obeys the rule of mean reversion. Say the average height of a person is 170 centimetres but both of your parents are 180 centimetres, it's likely that your height will be somewhere between 180 centimetres and 170 centimetres. Why? Because of the tendency to revert to the average.

The same thing happens regularly with corporates. Companies that have been very successful and pull ahead of their competitors tend to come back to the middle of the field over a long period of time. This occurs for a whole range of reasons. For instance, it's very difficult to sustain above average sales growth over an extended period because your competition are unlikely to take that lying down. Similarly, it's hard to deliver excessive returns in perpetuity because again, competition comes into play. Over a shorter time horizon a premium return may be possible, because it can take time for the competition to catch up with you due to the advantages you've created that we discussed in the Strategic Analysis section above.

A case in point, and one seen regularly, is where a company expects its returns on capital will increase much more significantly in the future than they ever have in the past. What this company is saying is that the market is going to let them make more money than they ever have before — and that's not a sustainable assumption. You are very unlikely to get away with smashing the competition over a long period of time because your competitors simply won't allow it — they will react.

So when putting together your financial forecasts, in order to make growth projections or projections of value drivers, it's important to be aware of trends that don't reflect mean reversion.

The final thing to consider in your financial analysis is to compare these value driver ratios against others in your industry. Why is this important? Benchmarking not only enables you to see where you've made unreasonable estimates of the future, but it also allows you work out where you're positioned in the industry right now. Are you sailing ahead of the rest of the pack, or drifting in the others' white water? Plus, what are the drivers of that?

You need to conduct a strategic analysis and a financial analysis in order to work out how much your business is worth. One without the other will only give you half the story. Combined, these two analyses will show where your business currently sits in terms of the economy, your industry, the company's current plans, its historical performance, its future performance and its competitors. This, in turn, sets you up nicely to begin valuing your business.

KEY TAKEAWAYS

→ A useful tool for assessing the industry your business resides in is Michael Porter's 'Five Forces' model for industry analysis and business strategy.

→ It's imperative you recognise that competitive positioning is dynamic. Your competitors are not going to stand around waiting for your next move any more than your customers are.

→ The strategic plans of your organisation are important because they provide a link between your competitive position now and your competitive position in the future.

→ Always do a Quality of Earnings Analysis to gain a realistic picture of your company's performance.

→ When forecasting, it's important to look for trends that don't reflect mean reversion.

FURTHER READING

Christopher Golis, *Enterprise and Venture Capital, A Business Builder's and Investor's Handbook (4th edition)*, Allen & Unwin, Crows Nest, 2002.

Michael Porter, *Competitive Strategy*, Free Press, New York, 1998.

David Besanks, David Dranove, Mark Shanley & Scott Schaeter, *Economics of Strategy (5th edition)*, Wiley & Sons, Hoboken, 2010.

Chapter 3

Basic valuation, discounted cash flows and multiples

*In our view, though, investment students need
only two well-taught courses — How to Value a
Business, and How to Think about Market Prices.*
— Warren Buffett, business magnate and investor

Warren Buffett (perhaps the doyen of investors) makes a statement about the importance of valuation education that receives no argument from me. Nor does his other well-known quote about valuation: 'Price is what you pay. Value is what you get.' I'd even agree with his more colourful line about risk that 'You only find out who is swimming naked when the tide goes out'.

However, I'd like to start this chapter with an idea Buffett has floated more than once (and one that was earlier popularised by economist Milton Friedman): 'In economics, there is no free lunch'.[14] The idea that there ain't no free lunches is more technically known in valuation circles as 'the law of one price'. This rule states that in an efficient market all identical goods must have only one price. Why? Because sellers will head for the highest market price, consumers will look for the lowest and the point at which the two converge will be the single, prevailing price.

Imagine you were trying to navigate your way through uncharted waters to find a particular location. One of the main skills in sailing is triangulating, by which sailors use two known locations to pinpoint a third, unknown position. The law of one price works in much the same way. Valuers use several techniques to navigate their way to one common market price.

This chapter examines the mechanics of valuation. There are three principal methods of valuation to choose from, but no matter which method you use, all are related to one another through this law of one price.

Traditional approaches to valuation

There are three principal approaches used to value equity, a business or an investment. These approaches are:

i) income method (what you expect to receive from an asset)
ii) market method (what you can sell the asset for)
iii) cost method (what it would cost to replace the asset).

The reason these three methods are all related through the law of one price is that, regardless of how good a return you might make on an asset, you'd never pay more for that asset than what you could buy it for elsewhere or more than what you could recreate it for.

Take a house, for example. Say it's an impressive house with that feature so revered by real estate agents — 'water glimpses'. If that house were going to cost you a million dollars, and if you could buy the block of land next door for just $500,000 and build a house on it for $200,000, you'd never pay a million for the first house. Even if the house in question were worth a lot to you personally, if you could buy it for less than you valued it at you'd never pay that asking price. (For a refresher on the distinction between price and value, see Chapter 1.)

However, over time this law of one price can get out of kilter. A perfect example of this is the internet boom of the late 1990s. At the end of the century people were paying enormous amounts of money for companies that cost almost nothing to recreate, thus violating the law of one price.

> Over time this law of one price can get out of kilter.

This was unsustainable over a long period of time, as history proved. A competitive market means that if it's ever possible to make significantly more money out of an asset than it costs to replace that asset, many people will create the asset in question and competition will recalibrate returns in that market. The market will move into some form of equilibrium. While this won't happen instantly (more likely, competition will restore equilibrium over a long period of time) it will happen almost every time.

But back to those three methods of valuation. To decide the most appropriate method for your situation, you should consider these two factors:

→ **Nature of item** — is the asset profitable? Does the asset have stable or fluctuating earnings? Where does the asset sit in terms of product lifecycle?

→ **Data availability and quality** — are forecasts prepared? Do comparative companies exist? How reliable are the assumptions?

To illustrate all three valuation techniques, let's walk through a fictional company called ValueIT Limited. ValueIT's financials are summarised below (I've used the old-fashioned names here as some habits are hard to break).

Profit and loss

	$M
Sales	250
EBITA	**75**
Depreciation	20
Amortisation	10
EBIT	**45**
Interest	6
Profit before tax	**39**
Tax	13
Profit after tax	**26**
Dividend	20
Retained profits	**6**

Balance Sheet

	$M
Cash	4
Receivables	72
Inventories	24
	100
Property, plant & equipment	120
Intangibles	100
	220
Total assets	**320**
Creditors, accruals & provisions	(40)
Interest-bearing liabilities	(100)
Total liabilities	**(140)**
Net assets	**180**

Cash flow statements

	$M
Profit after tax	26
Movement in working capital	5
Depreciation & amortisation	30
Operating cash flows	**61**
Investing cash flows	
Capital expenditure	(36)
Financing cash flows	
Dividends	(20)
Net cash flows	**5**

Market statistics

	$M
Market capitalisation	400
No. of shares	2
Share price	30

Income method of valuation

The income method of valuation is based on what you expect to receive from an asset, and the most common way to carry out the income method is by using discounted cash flows (DCF). Valuation is calculated by estimating a stream of future earnings, cash flows or asset values and then discounting these to a present value.

So how are estimated future earnings discounted?

This involves forming a probability-weighted view of the future (i.e. what you expect the future to be like, on average, for cash inflows) and then discounting those back at the weighted average cost of capital (WACC).

Here it's worth pointing out that it's not enough to simply take an optimistic view of the future and then discount it back. Your DCF should be 'the average of the future'. This way, you'll avoid the common mistake of a valuation that's possible, but not probable.

Take, for example, a US court case around a power plant development proposal in the Asia-Pacific region that one of my partners was involved in. A key point in this case was the DCF value of a power plant that had not been built but was an approved proposal. During the case, it was pointed out that for every proposal like that of the power plant, several more proposals in that particular region never saw the light of day. As soon as these other failed developments were taken into consideration, the weighted average probability of the power plant coming into existence was considerably less (and thus the DCF value was much lower) and the court case in question was won on this single salient point.

To return to the WACC for a moment, it needs to account for the time value of money and risk, and risk is all about the future.

But before we jump too far into the future, let's pause for a bit of history about allowing for risk. Back in 1955 US economist Harry Markowitz received a PhD from the University of Chicago for his thesis on portfolio theory. So radical were his ideas at the time that fellow economist Milton Friedman argued his contribution didn't fall under the banner of economics at all. Markowitz's thesis? Portfolio theory states that when you buy one share it's quite risky, but when you buy all the shares, this evens out the risk. What this tells us is that it's much less risky to hold a portfolio of assets rather than just one. Markowitz's insight adds much to our understanding of the cost of capital and, in turn, DCF.

When determining the cost of capital, it's normally assumed that the asset in question will be added to an already well-diversified portfolio. This is usually estimated by the capital asset pricing model (CAPM). This model takes into account the asset's sensitivity to non-diversifiable risk (or systemic risk), rather than the risk of the individual assets, in giving the discount rate to be applied to future cash flows. Where cash flows are on an ungeared basis — as is most common — the appropriate cost of capital is the WACC.

The diagram below illustrates the underlying assumptions in calculating the WACC (i.e. that business risk is dependent on the weighing of debt and equity and the associated risk premiums).

Figure 10: Calculating the WACC

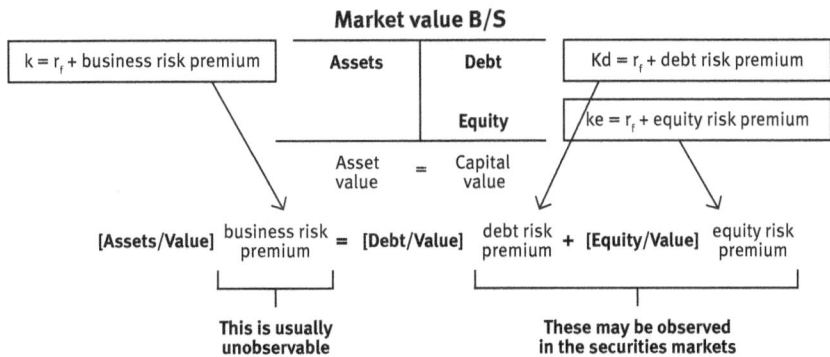

A DCF analysis for ValueIT shows the most common approach of nominal un-geared cash flows:

Free cash flows

	$M
Profit after tax	26
Add:	
Interest	6
Depreciation & amortisation	30
Movement in working capital	5
Deduct:	
Capital expenditure	(36)
Tax shield on interest	(2)
Free cash flows	**29**

We have excluded the cash flow value of imputation credits for simplicity here.[15]

DCF valuation

	02/03	03/04	04/05	05/06	Terminal
FCF	29	33	38	40	45
Terminal multiple					14
Future value	29	33	38	40	630
Discount factor	0.917	0.842	0.772	0.708	0.649
Present value	27	28	29	28	409
Enterprise value	**521**				
Debt	(100)				
Equity value	**421**				
WACC assumed to be 9%					

Under the income method, it is extremely important that the basis of fore-casting is consistent throughout. For instance, will cash flows be on a real or nominal basis (with or without the impact of inflation)? Will they be geared or ungeared? What is the forecasting period over which cash flows are to be analysed? What do you expect will happen to the business at the end of this period? Should a terminal cash flow value be calculated? Naturally, a DCF re-lies on a great number of behavioural, accounting and other assumptions, so consistency is key.

The advantages and disadvantages of the income approach are:

Advantages	Disadvantages
→ Value driver assumptions are explicit → Growth duration period is explicitly modelled → Can incorporate lumpy cash flows → Useful for turnaround businesses, especially those not currently making a profit	→ Difficult to assess value driver projections objectively, leading to 'j-curve' (or hockey stick) outcomes → Period of growth difficult to get objective data on → Significant amounts of value in the terminal value (which is usually very sensitive to changes in assumptions!)

Market method of valuation

As the name suggests, the market method uses market prices of comparable assets to work out what your own asset is valued at. Sounds simple, doesn't it? In reality, it's a little more complex. For a start, the market data used is objective data, but selecting assets that are comparable to your own (in terms of growth, risk and return) is a subjective exercise and requires skill.

Moreover the market method of assessing value is talking about price. By using the price of similar assets on the market to work out the worth of your own asset, it's really price that is being determined. Not value. It's only value if you're a speculator and you want to gamble on price movements. The market method doesn't fully adhere to the definition of value that we covered earlier; it could more accurately be described as a way of estimating price.

Semantics aside, let's run through some common multiples used in the market method. The most common multiples and the application valuation outcome are shown below for ValueIT. For example, a two-times multiple of sales provides the enterprise value of $500 million compared to a 15-times multiple of NPAT (which gives the equity value of $400 million).

	Financials		Values	
	$m	Market Cap	Debt	Enterprise Value
		400	100	500
			Multiples	
Sales	250			2
EBITA	75			7
EBIT	45			11
NPAT	26	15		
Dividends	20	5%		
Net assets	180	2		
Net tangible assets	80	5		
Capital employed	280			2

(Note: these multiples have been rounded for simplicity.)

This can be quite confusing because if someone mentions a particular result is a multiple of 15, what multiple are they talking about? Practitioners and commentators often use different multiples seemingly interchangeably. Add to this that sometimes multiples are quotes on a historical basis (such as, a multiple of last year's earnings to value); or as a forward multiple (think: What are next year's earnings predicted to be compared to value?), and you can sail into trouble.

This is not intended to overwhelm you. The point is simply that it's important to understand which multiple is being talked about. Always quantify which basis for comparison is being used, as well as which basis of time. In a nutshell, do I have the right multiple and the right time frame?

As a guide, the following table summarises the median and quartile multiples for the ASX 200 at 24 January 2011 (sourced from Capital IQ).

Historical	1st quartile	Median	3rd quartile
Revenue	1.1	2.5	6.2
EBITDA	6.5	9.5	12.5
EBIT	10.2	13.2	17.7
PE	13.5	17.2	24.7
Dividend Yield	0.0%	3.1%	6.5%
NTA	1.3	2.8	6.5

It's also worth remembering that these multiples are not stable over time. See, for example, the path of the revenue multiple for the ASX 200 over the last five years.

Figure 11: Spreadsheet showing the trend of the ASX 200 and its revenue multiple[16]

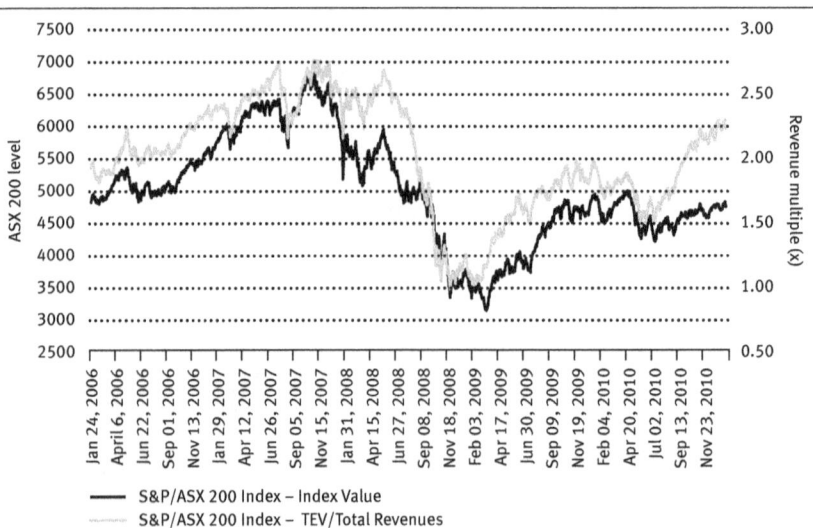

S&P/ASX 200 Index – Index Value
S&P/ASX 200 Index – TEV/Total Revenues

All up, the advantages and the disadvantages of the market approach to valuation are:

Advantages	Disadvantages
→ Market based → Does not rely on optimistic forecasts → Does not require detailed forecasting → Simple mechanics	→ Subject to market hubris → Value driver assessments going forward are implied and not explicit → Comparability difficult to establish → Often distorted by market issues (e.g. illiquidity of stock)

> The strategic plans of your organisation are important because they provide a link between your competitive position now and your competitive position in the future.

Asset- or cost-based method

The final approach to valuation — the asset- or cost-based approach — looks at the fair market value of each of the individual assets and liabilities of an entity to determine the total value of the business. The asset approach asks: What is the replacement cost of the asset or the sales cost of individual pieces? More often than not, this method is used when the business is not generating enough income to support its assets, or in the case of businesses (such as research and development companies) that are not seeing a profit now but expect to in the future.

> In terms of financial results, there are three components which are relevant: historical performance, forecast performance and relative performance or benchmarks.

Key to this approach is the idea that if it costs $1 million to replace an asset but you can only ever make $1 out of that asset, it's only ever worth $1. It's always important to come back to the law of one price whenever you use these techniques.

The asset-based approach can use one of two bases:

i) **Continued-use basis** — this calculates the value of assets and liabilities as if they were used in a systematic way, without time limitations or purchase constraints. This basis is used where the item valued will continue to operate into the future.

ii) **Liquidation basis** — under this basis the assets and liabilities are valued under forced sale conditions (or in some cases a more orderly realisation assumption is used). Typically, a forced sale will command a discount and, therefore, a liquidation basis gives a lower value to assets than continued-use basis. The liquidation basis is used if it's expected that the business will stop operating in the near future.

ValueIT's numbers are useful in illustrating the outcomes that are likely under the two bases:

Value of assets	Existing	Liquidation
Cash	4	4
Receivables	72	70
Inventories	40	30
Creditors, accruals & provisions	(40)	(45)
Property, plant & equipment	120	60
Brand	200	41
Other non-identified intangibles (incl. goodwill)	125	-
Debt	(100)	(100)
	421	60

The advantages and disadvantages are as follows:

Advantages	Disadvantages
→ Straightforward → Easy to reconcile with financial statements → Provides breakdown of value by asset type, which can be reconciled to underlying market values in secondary markets → Particularly relevant for pure investment companies or in cases of poor performance and/or financial distress	→ Often relies on other valuation techniques to generate stand-alone asset values → Limited applicability as a primary technique for companies in growth mode or those that are economically profitable

Crosscheck or capsize

Perhaps the most valuable piece of advice I ever received for carrying out a valuation — and the best way to avoid capsizing your results — is to crosscheck by using more than one of the methods outlined. This is especially the case if you're planning to use the income approach with discounted cash flows. The DCF process has up to 15 or 16 inputs so even if you get most of these inputs spot on, any miscalculations can add up and your results will be out of whack.

KEY TAKEAWAYS

→ All three methods of valuation are related through the law of one price, or the notion of a single price point.

→ When carrying out a DCF, it should be probability weighted. It's not enough to take an optimistic view of the future and then discount it back. Your DCF should be 'the average of the future'; this way you'll avoid arriving at a valuation that's possible, but not probable.

→ It's also important to check which basis for comparison is being used, as well as which basis of time. In a nutshell, do I have the right multiple and the right time frame?

→ Finally, it's good to cross check your results by using a couple of different valuation methods.

FURTHER READING

Tom Copeland, Tim Koller and Jack Murrin, *Valuation: Measuring and Managing the Value of Companies (3rd edition)*, John Wiley & Sons Ltd, New York, 2000.

Aswath Damodaran, *Damodaran on Valuation*, Baker & Taylor, New York, 1994.

Wayne Lonergan, *The Valuation of Businesses, Shares and Other Equity*, Allen & Unwin, Crows Nest, 2003.

Tim Ogier, John Rugman and Lucinda Spicer, *The Real Cost of Capital*, Pearson Education, London, 2004.

Chapter 4

Advanced techniques: residual income

and real options

Do not repeat the tactics which have gained you one victory,
but let your methods be regulated by the infinite variety of
circumstances.
— Sun Tzu (c. 490 BC), Chinese military strategist

On 22 August 1851, Britain's time as the world's undisputed maritime ruler ended. Commodore John Cox Stevens from the upstart New York Yacht Club (NYYC) sailed the radical-looking schooner *America* around the Isle of Wight and to victory, winning the Royal Yacht Squadron's £100 Cup. Faced with wind and rain (not to mention Britain's intimidating naval history), the New York challengers were forced to sail to the conditions on the day. Just as you don't put a spinnaker up in a head wind just because you won the last race with it, the *America* crew had to think on their feet to cope with the conditions on the day.

Whatever the 1851 equivalent of a winged keel was, it must have worked for the Americans. To the astonishment of the watching Queen Victoria, *America* beat all 15 yachts of the British Royal Yacht Squadron, becoming the first recipient of what is now known as The America's Cup.

On seeing *America* cross the finish line, Queen Victoria is reported to have asked who was coming second. With no other yacht in sight — and as a good reminder to us that success depends on behaving according to circumstance — the now-famous reply came: 'Your majesty, there is no second.'

This same rule of circumstance applies for exceptional or unusual industries in business. For instance, how do mining magnates apply valuation techniques to their circumstances, when so many of their tenements end up uneconomic? How do research and development companies value their businesses when they're investing millions of dollars in ideas with no guarantee they'll ever work?

In such situations, there are a couple of advanced valuation techniques available — residual income and real options — and we'll explore both in this chapter. Both techniques work well in certain circumstances and both add much to our understanding of valuation.

Residual income

Residual income is living proof that everything old is new again. It's an old technique first developed by Alfred Sloan, the long-time president of business leviathan General Motors and the namesake of the Alfred P. Sloan School of Management (one of the world's premier business schools).

Sloan argued that it's not enough to just assess profit; rather, you have to assess profit after calculating the cost of capital tied up in developing that profit. This is the definition of residual income: profit after the cost of equity capital.

The concept of residual income has been rebranded and popularised several times since Sloan. In the late 1980s a small New York consulting organisation called Stern Stewart & Co. touted a new valuation technique named 'Economic Value Added'; essentially, this was no different from Sloan's original residual income idea. Similarly, Boston Consulting Group's (BCG) 'Cash Flow Return on Investment' owes much to Sloan.

Regardless of what you call it, residual income is a popular idea.

Why? Because residual income is a really useful way of determining the value of mature assets, especially assets that have received large amounts of capital investment.

But the real beauty of residual income is that it's an excellent crosschecking device. Remember how I mentioned that there were lots of inputs and, therefore, lots of opportunities for things to go wrong in a DCF? Well, residual income prevents us from overestimating the amount of excess return (in fact, it almost constrains us) because its focus is on the amount of excess return.

Residual income is an economically based method of valuation, because the expectation is that, over the long term, residual income will be zero. Cast your mind back to all those wonderful graphs depicting perfect competition that you would have drawn in Economics 101. You were always taught that in a perfectly competitive market, profits would be zero, right? (That means economic profits, not profits in the traditional sense of the word — making that distinction clarified a great confusion for me in Economics 101!) This rule applies here.

One person who does understand the importance of residual income is Qantas CEO Alan Joyce. Joyce demonstrated as much in recent times when he announced Qantas's plans to revamp its international operations in a bid to regain market share and decrease its dependence on the carrier's budget unit, Jetstar. In an interview, Joyce conceded Qantas 'isn't returning its cost of capital, and the other businesses have been compensating for it for some time. That can't continue, and we need it to grow'.[17]

So how do you go about calculating residual income? Basically, you need to work out profit after tax and then deduct a capital charge for the equity capital that's invested. There are a couple of ways of doing this.

Residual income to equity

Residual income charges profitability with the cost of employing shareholder funds. The rate at which funds are charged is generally the cost of the equity (i.e. the return expected by shareholders). Let's use ValueIT's numbers again:

Residual income

	$M
Net profit after tax	26
Less:	
Capital charge	(18)
Residual income	8

Capital charge	
Net assets	180
@ cost of equity	10%

To get a value from this calculation, economists show that the sum of the shareholders' funds plus the present value of future residual income equals the current value of the business.[18]

Economic profitability

This is residual income to all security holders and is the same concept as residual income to equity but extended to all sources of capital.

Despite being popular in academic circles, the concept of residual income is less common in practice, except perhaps in management valuations where it's often used for incentive plan design. In these situations, companies work out the residual income for each period and then incentivise executives to increase this amount. That's predominantly how Stern Stewart used the concept. They promoted residual income as a way of incentivising management and aligning management and shareholders more closely, in order to achieve a better outcome for shareholders.

But there are a whole bunch of issues to consider when using residual income in this way. For instance, one of the great lessons from the GFC was that when it comes to executives, short-term measures of performance — especially those that favour risk taking — aren't such a flash idea. Examples such as Lehman Brothers are a good reminder that it's better to ensure executives don't get paid out before the ills they create come to rest. So when using a residual income approach, a long-term focus is recommended.

Because residual income is ultimately a function of DCF, it has similar advantages and disadvantages, shown here.

Advantages	Disadvantages
→ Value driver assumptions are explicit → Growth duration period is explicitly modelled with parameters used to return drivers to overall averages (in the case of CFROI) → Reduces the terminal value by focusing on the investment base → Same theoretical underpinnings as DCF	→ Period of growth difficult to get objective data on → Typical economic value added and residual income applications subject to same J-curve as DCF → Most relevant to businesses with substantial assets in place (about 75% of the corporate population) → Increased complexity of adjustments reduces transparency for users of DCF → Limited consideration of risk other than in the discount rate

Real options

Another advanced technique is real option valuation (ROV). ROV is usually for businesses at the other end of the life cycle: in start-up phase, when failure — and conversely, the success opportunity — are both high risk.

> Always check which multiple is being used, as well as which time period this applies to.

Real options talk about the value of information. It's an extension of two aspects of financial thought — DCF and option valuation, where option valuation recognises the benefit of being able to wait to see how things turn out before making your investment decision. Removing the risk from decision-making, if you will.

Think of it like this. One of the biggest gambles in sailing, strangely, is deciding whether you should even get the boat out of the shed. When you factor in how much time and energy (not to mention money) it takes to get a boat ready, you want to make sure you're going to get a good day's sailing in return for your investment. So how much would you pay to know, for certain, what the weather will be like in advance? What is the value of that information to you?

The real option method of valuation recognises that if conditions change, management reactions will also change.

So the value of real options is that you get to learn before you act.

How does ROV differ from DCF (and similar techniques)?

DCF	→ **Static** — addresses fixed conditions → **Deterministic** — uses a single forecast or limited treatment of uncertainty through the use of scenario planning/sensitivities → **Inflexible; ignores optionality** — relies on a single business case that ignores the flexibility to act in response to uncertain changing conditions
ROV	→ **Dynamic** — responds to changing conditions → **Probabilistic** — incorporates more complete consideration of uncertainty through events and probabilities → **Flexible; captures optionality** –incorporates a business plan that captures flexibility to act in response to uncertain changing conditions

The advantages and disadvantages of real options can be summarised as follows.

Advantages	Disadvantages
→ Builds on advantages of DCF modelling → Incorporates management reactions to certain events → Real options have value only if a competitive advantage exists; this allows qualitative rigour in the analysis → Promotes deeper understanding of strategic options	→ Difficult to assess real option projections objectively, leading to J-curve outcomes → Option valuation techniques used to value financial options do not apply well because their fundamental assumptions (assumptions about price behaviour and liquid markets in the underlying asset) do not always exist) → More complex and less frequently used, making stakeholder discussions more difficult

As we began discussing earlier in the chapter, there are several types of industries that can and do use real options. Industries where there are high levels of risk or opportunity to manage (such as the mining industry or R&D industries), or where there are multiple stages to production, such as the film industry. Some film production companies, for instance, use real options to calculate how likely it is that any one script will give results. For an industry where most investments will result in a loss — but where a win could mean seriously big money — real options is a great technique for working out value.

A simple example to illustrate real options is by contrasting the following coin tosses.

Say you're going to bet $1 on the flip of a coin. Depending on where you got the coin, you've got a 50/50 chance of winning and if you call correctly on a $1 bet, you receive $2. So what would you pay for that bet? Simple. You'd bet 50 per cent of $2 (or $1). That's the 'actuarial' value of the bet. In practice, because many people are more sensitive to losses than gains, the market value of the bet might be lower, as we discuss later.

That is the basic coin toss. The real option is the same game with a twist. We're still talking about a $1 bet and we're still talking about a 50/50 chance of winning but the real option twist is that you can now wait till the coin has been flipped and has stopped moving — just before it falls on one side — to place your bet.

Why would you pay for the right to wait to place your $1 bet?

It seems like value is coming from nothing, right? Not quite, because you are paying for the extra information that you get by waiting until the coin falls. You'd probably pay up to 50 cents. If you could get someone to agree to this somewhat contrived game, you'd have a real option.

Graphically, the contrast between the early bet and the real option value looks like this.

Figure 12: Coin toss comparison

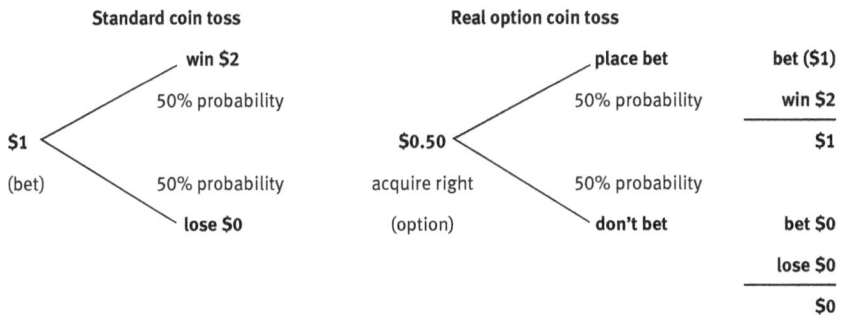

In reality, as always, it's not quite so simple. If you were indifferent about winning or losing 50 cents that's exactly how things would pan out; however, we have to take into account one (not insignificant) aspect of human behaviour called risk aversion.

Risk aversion is an idea that's been explored by behavioural economists such as Richard H. Thaler. It explains the reluctance of a person to accept a bargain with an uncertain payoff, compared to a bargain with a more certain but possibly lower payoff. Thaler and co have worked out that we value losses about twice as much as we value gains.

In our example, you'd probably pay 25 cents rather than 50 cents assuming you, like Thaler's subjects, value the loss twice as much as you value the gain (assuming the value in question were a meaningful amount to you — for instance, you're going to be more cavalier with 50 cents than you are with $50,000).

It's interesting to note that in this area of loss aversion the relative magnitude of the losses is important, too. Take the lottery, for example. The principle at play here is similar to that of the coin toss. Only we don't pay a fair bet to enter the lottery (such as $1); instead we pay $1.10 or so (i.e. a margin of 10 cents). Why? Because the prospect of a large gain is worth so much more to us than a small loss.

Rules and exceptions

Real option valuation is prevalent in those sorts of industries where profit is a bit of a gamble, particularly where the distribution of value outcomes is highly skewed. Residual income, which we covered earlier, assumes that there's as much chance of profit being higher as there is of it being lower, so profits are generally evenly distributed and most likely close to normalcy.

Also worth noting is that a DCF is pretty much useless where profit is a gamble. As we have discovered, DCF talks about the average of the future. In industries where value outcomes are highly skewed, the DCF is going to be zero or negative, except in some cases, where it's really positive. In these cases DCF doesn't work nearly so well.

KEY TAKEAWAYS

→ The two techniques of advanced valuation — residual income and real options — each work best in specific circumstances.

→ Residual income works well in regard to mature, well-established businesses.

→ Real options work well in situations where there's a lot of uncertainty, particularly where it's likely you'll make a loss and, occasionally, a significant profit.

→ Residual income is particularly useful in making sure you don't run away with your assumptions, which is easy to do with a DCF.

→ Real options focus very heavily on the value of information, and the value of flexibility in responding to that information.

FURTHER READING

Thomas E. Copeland and Vladimir Antikarov, *Real Options: A Practitioner's Guide*, Texere, New York, 2003.

G. Bennett Stewart III, *The Quest for Value: A Guide for Senior Managers*, HarperCollins, New York, 1991.

Dan Ariely, *Predictably Irrational, Revised and Expanded Edition: The Hidden Forces that Shape our Decisions*, HarperCollins, New York, 2009.

Arthur S. De Vany, *Hollywood Economics: How Extreme Uncertainty Shapes the Film Industry (Routledge Studies in Contemporary Political Economy)*, Routledge, London, 2004.

Chapter 5

Special circumstances: R&D,

mining and financial services

Never underestimate the power of a simple tool.
— Craig Bruce, Canadian software developer

Surprising as it may seem, when I think about industry-specific valuation, I think about dinghy sailing. The two have quite a bit in common.

Although I haven't been in a dinghy since I was a kid, the mechanics of sailing a simple dinghy are exactly the same as for a larger boat. Same sails, same general layout; in fact, the only differences between the two types of sailing are the techniques used. For example, while many larger boats have a fixed keel, a dinghy has a centreboard that makes your weight (as an individual) much more important to the way the boat sails. This is why you'll often seen people on board a dinghy leaning out the side, precariously balanced on a trapeze. Because a dinghy is so much smaller than a cruising yacht, it's also much less steady to sail — a description that could just as easily apply to industries with exceptional valuation characteristics, such as research and development (R&D), mining and financial services.

These industries have different practices that have developed because of the particular economics of the industries that differ from 'standard' industries. So, just as you use different techniques to sail a dinghy, in this chapter we look at the different techniques used to value in these special circumstances. While we don't do anything as dramatic as hanging out the side of a boat on a trapeze, the techniques used in this chapter range from subtly to dramatically different when compared with basic valuations. The trick is to work out which technique is right for your situation.

Early stage or R&D investments

Traditionally, Australians are under-investors in new technology. Although the Australian Bureau of Statistics (ABS) reports that business spending on R&D totalled $12.1 billion in 2006-07 (an increase of 11.8 per cent in real terms over the previous year), we still spend much less on R&D than the OECD average.[19]

> Perhaps the most valuable piece of advice I ever received for carrying out a valuation is to cross-check by using more than one method.

We don't have a very active venture capital community (even relatively speaking) when compared to somewhere like the US, and many Australians find themselves compelled to head to places like the States for start-up or growth funding. Part of the reason for this is that we just don't have asset allocations that feed into 'risky' ventures, and this can be put down to the value dynamic I outline below. Basically, most early-stage investments will see you lose your money. It's only occasionally that you won't, meaning you need to have a lot of bets on the table to be well-placed to win and there just aren't that many available within our economy.

> Both advanced valuation techniques — residual income and real options — work well in particular circumstances.

Yet these tables may slowly be turning. R&D may still be a much smaller industry in Australia than giants such as mining and financial services, but our spending on R&D (as a proportion of gross domestic product) has increased for the past seven successive years.[20] Which is one reason why the valuation approach to new opportunities is now starting to get interesting. After all, the value of new ideas is the value of our future.

Valuing an opportunity: why early stage valuation is different

The difference between early-stage investments, such as R&D investments, and more standard forms of investment is essentially twofold: first, most R&D ventures fail; and second, on the off-chance that your venture doesn't fail, then the returns can be phenomenal.

Take Google for example. When the first funding for Google was secured in August 1998, Andy Bechtolsheim, co-founder of Sun Microsystems, stumped up US$100,000 to get things off the ground. By 2010, Google's IPO was US$23.1 billion and, at the time of writing, the company had a market value of US$177.2 billion[21] and Bechtolsheim was laughing all the way to the bank. But for every Google success story there are countless examples of R&D ventures that fail, making valuation of early-stage investments more complex and risky than for mature businesses.

Aside from heightened risk and (potentially) heightened returns, what else is different about early-stage investment? A few factors are at play here:

→ zero value is a likely (and even the most common) case
→ in the words of Louis B. Mayer: 'Nobody knows anything'
→ early-stage investments are not generally liquid or transparent
→ there is often no cash generation for many years
→ vendors are optimistic and buyers mostly pessimistic, creating vast bid–ask differences.

As you can see, zero value is the most likely valuation, which makes traditional DCF unappealing. Remember I mentioned that with DCF valuations, we're trying to work out the average of the future? With early-stage investments, the average of the future is often zero, rendering the traditional DCF valuation useless.

As for Louis B. Mayer's advice that 'Nobody knows anything', it's a fine principle to work to, but it's also worth remembering that there is tremendous uncertainty, not just risk, associated with early-stage investments. You see, risk is just the variability of outcomes possible. For instance, when you play blackjack, there's risk involved but you know what that risk is: you know how many cards are in the deck and you know what the odds are of each card coming out. With risk, you don't know what's going to come next but you do know what the parameters are.

Uncertainty is different. Using our blackjack example, uncertainty would be like playing with an infinitely shuffled deck of cards so you have no way of knowing how many cards are in the deck. Here, there's not just risk (or variability) but there's the added complication of not knowing what the parameters are. When valuing R&D ventures, you'll do well to remember that, really, nobody knows anything. Least of all how many cards are in the deck.

Valuing early stage investments
There are two approaches to valuing R&D.

1. Venture capital approach
This approach asks what a mature business would look like, using a DCF model of valuation, then accounts for the risk associated with an early-stage investment by using a higher discount rate. In this way, the venture capital approach recognises that the probability of an early-stage venture reaching maturity is less than for an already mature business. The discounted rate for required returns at each stage of the development life cycle is outlined in the graph below. Here you can see how the discount rate decreases as product development progresses.

Figure 13: Value dynamics through a life cycle[22]
Discount rates for required returns (extracted from Stanford lecture):

Phase	Seed	Start-up	First Stage	2nd Stage + Bridge	Public (IPO)	Public (Mature)
Fundning source	Founder sweat equity	Angels – close associates	Angels VC	VC	Public	Public
Investment stage	Inception	Concept validation	Technology validation	Market validation	Expansion	Cash generative
Discount rate	80%+	50-70%	30-60%	20-50%	10-25%	7-15%

2. Real options approach

The second model for valuing early-stage investments is one we looked at last chapter: real options valuation. This method is far more specific about what is driving the risk at each stage of development, whereas the venture capital ap-proach is a more generalised, rule-of-thumb approach.

Because the real options approach to valuation is already spelled out in Chapter 4 (including a worked example), I won't run through it in detail again here. Instead, an example follows showing how to use the venture capital method.

Before looking at that example, keep in mind that there are six key questions that need to be answered before you can value an early stage investment:

i)   What do mature businesses in the industry sector trade at?
ii)   How could this opportunity change the market fundamentals?
iii) How long is the development cycle?
iv) How large are the risks at each stage of investment?
v)   What is the capital requirement at each stage?
vi) What cost has the developer incurred?

With those six questions in your mind, take a look at this example of the ven-ture capital approach to valuation.

Figure 14: A worked example of how to use the venture capital method

Discount rate	80%	50%	30%	20%		Mature fundamentals
Post-money	0.5	5.0	20.0	80.0	100.0	1,000 Market size
Capital required	(0.1)	(2.0)	(10.0)	(50.0)		x
Pre-money	0.4	3.0	10.0	30.0		10% Market share
Replacement cost (weighted by success probability)	0.1	2.1	12.1	62.1		x
						10% Margins
						x
						10 x Market multiple
	1	2	3	4	5	

Life stage

To explain this analysis it is useful to start at the bottom and work backwards. Firstly the VC estimates how a mature business in the relevant market would be valued. I've made some broad assumptions in this example. They then discount this by the life-stage discount rate and the time for the stage. This gives the value after the stage 5 investment (post-money). Of course, if you are investing to fund the stage 5 then you need to deduct the value of the investment required. (This is known as a pre-money value.) VCs also compare this estimate to a replacement cost including a developer profit reflecting the probability of passing through each life stage. For an even earlier stage investment, the process is just iterated for each earlier stage.

As you can see, carrying out a valuation for an early-stage investment is a whole different ball game from valuing a standard industrial, so it makes sense that the valuation techniques used should be different too.

Mining investments

The second 'special circumstance' industry worth examining is the mining industry. Although, when you consider there were a massive 240 transactions worth $41.1 billion in the Australian mining, oil and gas sector in 2009 alone, this industry looks more like the norm than a special circumstance in Australia. Indeed, the biggest company in Australia is a mining company — BHP Billiton — and its local operations alone are worth more than our big four banks combined,[23] demonstrating just how significant mining is to our economy.

Given its significance, how do we attribute value in the mining industry? The curious art of valuation in mining is no more obvious than in the case of Nathan Tinkler. Tinkler, an electrician and businessman from Newcastle, got into the mining game when he borrowed $500,000 to buy a coal mine in which others saw no potential. One year later Tinkler sold his company to Macarthur Coal for $275 million. Four years on, Tinkler has amassed a $610 million mining fortune and enjoys being BRW's wealthiest Australian under 40. Not bad for an original outlay of $500,000.

That's the interesting thing about valuing a mining development. A basic, unexplored tenement can go from being a patch of dirt to an immensely valuable investment almost overnight, once it's proven to contain saleable, extractable commodities. It's not that the asset has changed in any way, only our knowledge and understanding of the asset, which is why information is so important when valuing a mine.

Stages of a mining development

There are three key stages within a mining development.

1. Exploration

A significant amount of geological exploration must take place to determine the potential of a mining tenement. Whether this is proven through drilling or seismic testing, there exists a whole framework around categorising geological information once it reaches the point of being classified as a 'resource' (i.e. its viability can be proven to a certain degree). This framework is provided by the Committee for Mineral Reserves International Reporting Standards (CRIRSCO) or the Joint Ore Reserves Committee (JORC) in Australia.

Figure 15: CRIRSCO classification of exploration results[24]

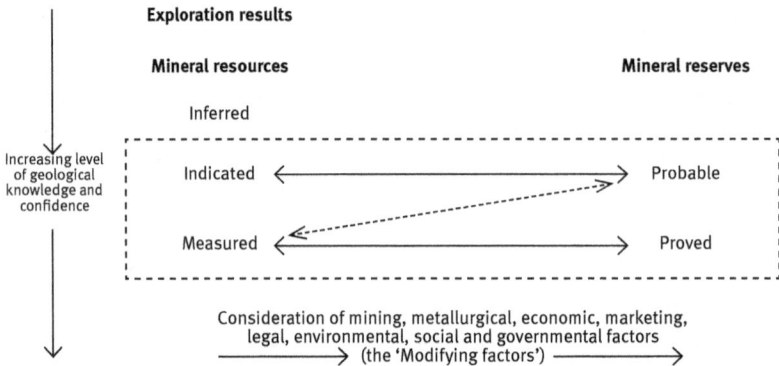

Most of the uncertainty associated with mining valuation occurs in the early stages of exploration. The chance that an unexplored tenement will go on to become a producing mine lies somewhere between one in 1000 and 10 in 100. Not great odds. But this is due to a whole range of factors, such as the accessibility of the mineral reserves, the access to transport, and demand (and therefore price) for the commodity. The fact that a mine proposal doesn't go ahead is not necessarily a reflection of what is or isn't in the ground.

But the probability of the development succeeding grows as you progress further through the mining process and as you find out more and more information about the mine. In fact, once you get to the later stages of development and production, mining is surprisingly easy to value. It's the preliminary stages, when a mine's success is far from guaranteed, that are hardest to put a figure on.

2. Development
Once you've progressed through the exploration stage and the mine has been classified as a mineral resource, mineral assets are divided into developing mines and producing mines. At the development stage, licenses need to be applied for in order for construction on the mine to begin.

     Most of the uncertainty associated with mining
     valuation occurs in the early stages of exploration.

> The chance that an unexplored tenement will go on to become a producing mine lies somewhere between one in 1000 and 10 in 100. Not great odds.

So how do we value a mining development? For mineral assets the three basic methods of valuation — the market approach, the income approach and the cost approach — can all be used. However, much like R&D, the skill is to know which valuation method to use when. Because each stage of the mining process works differently, and because each stage is (generally) less risky than the last, different valuation techniques apply for different stages.

Figure 16: Which valuation approach to use?

Valuing mining assets – valuation approaches

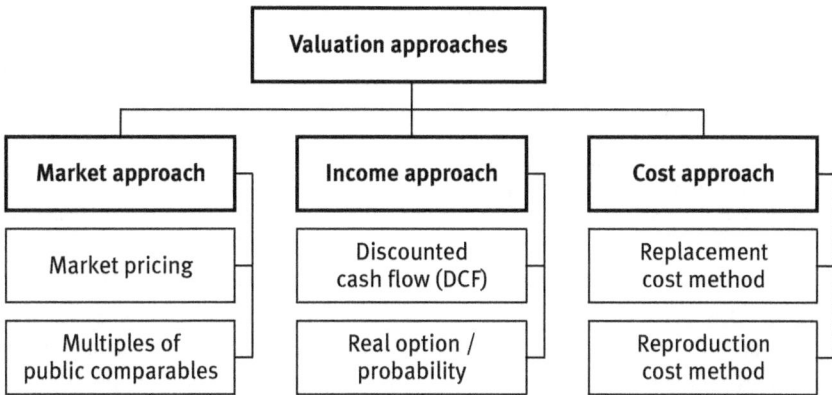

Valuation approach	Exploration	Mineral resource	Development	Production
Market	Yes	Yes	Yes	Yes
Income	Unlikely	In some cases	Yes	Yes
Cost	Yes	In some cases	No	No

3. Production
Once the mine shifts into production mode, it's relatively easy to value. Just like any other business, for an operating mine you should consider:

→ What's the operational plan? How do you intend to extract the commodity?

→ What's the cost of the capital employed?

→ How much can I sell the business for if I choose to do so?

A more extensive summary of value drivers is set out in the illustration on the following page.

Figure 17: Summary of value considerations[25]

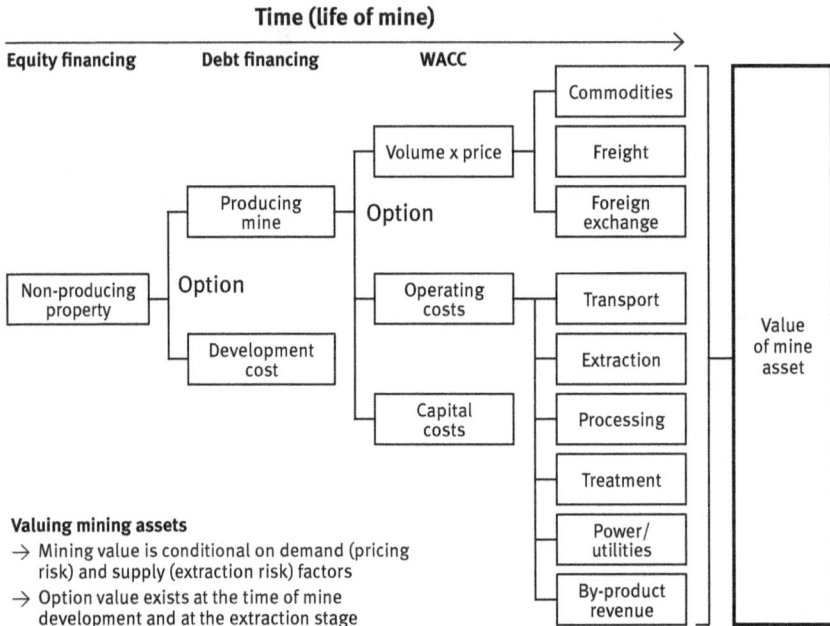

Time (life of mine)

| Equity financing | Debt financing | WACC |

```
                                                          ┌─ Commodities
                                        ┌─ Volume x price ─┼─ Freight
                    ┌─ Producing mine   │   Option         └─ Foreign
 Non-producing      │                   │                     exchange
 property   Option  │                   │                  ┌─ Transport
                    │                   ├─ Operating costs ─┼─ Extraction     Value
                    └─ Development cost │                   ├─ Processing     of mine
                                        │                   ├─ Treatment      asset
                                        └─ Capital costs    ├─ Power/
                                                            │   utilities
                                                            └─ By-product
                                                                revenue
```

Valuing mining assets
→ Mining value is conditional on demand (pricing risk) and supply (extraction risk) factors
→ Option value exists at the time of mine development and at the extraction stage

It's worth noting that a mine operator does enjoy some elbow room. For instance, if the price of the commodity you're mining dips below the cost of pulling it out of the ground, you can simply stop operating the mine until commodity prices recover because a mine is a relatively flexible asset. It is possible to leave a mine non-operational for a long period of time, in a way that you could never hope to mothball a factory. In Queensland, there are plenty of examples of old mines that are now being reworked because, with commodity price rises, they're suddenly viable again, or because mining technology advancements mean it's easier and cheaper to extract the minerals.

> A mine operator does enjoy some elbow room. For instance, if the price of the commodity you're mining dips below the cost of pulling it out of the ground, you can simply stop operating the mine until commodity prices recover because a mine is a relatively flexible asset.

Here is a worked example of how a producing mine is valued. As you can see, while an early-stage mining development poses some challenges for valuation, by the time a mine reaches development, fairly standard methods of valuation apply.

Figure 18: DCF valuation of a copper mineral property

Valuation of Mineral Property	20X9	20Y0	20Y1	20Y2	20Y3	20Y4	20Y5	20Y6	20Y7	20Y8
	1	2	3	4	5	6	7	8	9	10
Reserves and Resources Data (MT 000's)										
Opening balance	300,000	275,000	240,000	195,000	150,000	115,000	80,000	50,000	30,000	15,000
Less: annual tonnes extracted	25,000	35,000	45,000	45,000	35,000	35,000	30,000	20,000	15,000	15,000
Closing balance	275,000	240,000	195,000	150,000	115,000	80,000	50,000	30,000	15,000	0
Copper head grade %	0.55%	0.55%	0.55%	0.53%	0.50%	0.50%	0.50%	0.40%	0.40%	0.37%
Processing (recovery) %	80%	80%	80%	80%	80%	80%	80%	80%	80%	80%
Annual payable metals production (M lbs)	242.5	339.5	436.5	420.6	308.6	308.6	264.6	141.1	105.8	97.9
Metal price assumption (Copper US$ per lb)	$ 1.50	$ 1.65	$ 1.75	$ 1.95	$ 2.00	$ 1.95	$ 1.85	$ 1.75	$ 1.75	$ 1.75
Foreign exchange rate (USD/AUD)	0.75	0.70	0.75	0.80	0.75	0.75	0.75	0.75	0.75	0.75
Operating costs, net of by-product revenue (AUD$ per lb)	$ 1.27	$ 1.36	$ 1.27	$ 1.19	$ 1.28	$ 1.47	$ 1.47	$ 1.47	$ 1.47	$ 1.47
In AUD$ millions										
Revenue	485.0	800.3	1,018.5	1,025.3	823.1	802.5	652.6	329.2	246.9	228.4
Operating costs, net of by-product revenue	307.2	460.8	552.9	499.5	395.1	452.7	388.0	206.9	155.2	143.6
	177.8	339.5	465.6	525.8	428.0	349.8	264.6	122.3	91.7	84.8
Cash taxes (at 30%)	53.4	101.9	139.7	157.7	128.4	104.9	79.4	36.7	27.5	25.5
Cash flow from mining property after tax	124.4	237.6	325.9	368.1	299.6	244.9	185.2	85.6	64.2	69.3
Less: capital expenditures	- 25.0	- 25.0	- 25.0	- 25.0	- 100.0	- 100.0	- 100.0	- 50.0	- 50.0	- 50.0
Decrease/increase in working capital	2.0	- 5.0	- 4.0	-	2.0	-	2.0	2.0	1.0	-
Discretionary cash flow – Reserves & Resources	101.4	207.6	296.9	343.1	201.6	144.9	87.2	37.6	15.2	9.3
Present value factor, assuming a discount rate of 10% for reserves and 15% for resources	0.9535	0.8668	0.7880	0.7164	0.4636	0.4031	0.3506	0.3048	0.2651	
	10.0%	10.0%	10.0%	10.0%	15.0%	15.0%	15.0%	15.0%	15.0%	15.0%
Present value of discretionary cash flows	96.7	180.0	234.0	245.8	107.5	67.2	35.1	13.2	4.6	2.5
Present value of discretionary cash flows from Reserves to 2012	756.4									
Present value of discretionary cash flows from Resources from 2013	230.1									
Total present value of mining property	986.5									
Less: Net working capital, excluding cash	- 36.5									
Less: Value of property, plant and equipment	- 100.0									
Value of the mineral interest	$ 850.0									

Financial services

The third and final industry to look at is the financial services sector. Like mining, banking and insurance represent a very big part of the Australian economy. In fact, of the top 20 companies in Australia, a quarter of them are financial services companies. The main difference between financial services and other businesses is that money is their stock in trade, making it more complex to analyse their value.

Typically, the market method or the income method of valuation is used. But not as we know them. Both require modifications before being applied to the banking sector.

The way the market method is used is to focus on two principal multiples, rather than the raft of earnings multiples (such as EBIT and EBITDA) that we used for commercial companies in Chapter 3. These other multiples don't apply to banks, again because we're talking about businesses that trade in money.

The two principal multiples used in financial services valuation are:

i)   price–book ratio (or market–book ratio)[26]

ii) price–earnings ratio.[27]

The first of these, the price–book ratio, looks at the accounting value of all assets versus the market value. With banks, because so many of their assets are held as money rather than inventory, this is actually quite a good proxy. The current value of assets is often highly correlated to their book value; the only difference between the two is any goodwill that needs to be factored in.

> With banks, so many of their assets are held as money rather than inventory.

So the market–book ratio works well for bankers and insurers in a single period model. In a DCF model, financial services companies use what's called a 'cash flow to equity' method, whereas most industrial companies use a free cash flow method (i.e. cash flows to both debt and equity). This is again because of the nature of financial services businesses whereby debt financing activities are core operating activities and not pure financing activities. Because loans are the bread and butter of banks it makes no sense to analyse them as part of the financing of the business, so we treat them separately.

PE multiples also work relatively well because the leverage and amortisation differences that cause such comparability problems in industrial companies do not apply to anywhere near the same extent. For example, various capital rules (such as the Basel banking accord) mean that leverage is much more tightly clustered than in industrial businesses.

The other big difference between financial services and other industries is their value drivers. The cash flow statement for an insurer would look like this:

Figure 19: Cash flow statement for an insurer

	Gross written premiums
Less:	change in unearned premium reserves
Less:	change in technical reserves
Less:	claims paid
Equals:	underwriting result
Plus:	investment returns
Less:	cash tax rate
Equals:	cash flow to company
Less:	investment in solvency cover
Equals:	cash flow to investor

These are often split by in-force or embedded (currently contracted business) and appraisal value (all future contracts).

Similarly, for a bank, the value drivers look something like this:

Figure 20: Value drivers for a bank

	Asset growth
Times:	Net interest margin
Plus:	Non-interest income
Less:	Loan losses
Less:	Operating expenses
Less:	CAPEX
Less:	Cash tax
Equals:	Cash flow to bank
Less:	Investment in regulatory capital
Equals:	Free cash flow to equity (investors)

As you can see, value drivers for a bank and an insurer are quite different from the value drivers we covered in earlier chapters. Within financial services, the valuation techniques such as DCF are the same as elsewhere, but the characteristics of the business are such that you need to understand their different value drivers and the subtly different way in which the techniques are applied.

Financial services have a whole different set of value drivers.

KEY TAKEAWAYS

→ In circumstances where a valuation is being carried out in an industry different from the norm, the valuation techniques used should also be different.

→ There are two approaches to valuing R&D companies: the venture capital approach and the real options approach. Both should be modified according to the characteristics of early stage investments.

→ For mineral assets, the three basic valuation methods can be used — the trick is to know when to use each method.

→ Typically, the market method or the income method of valuation is used for financial services. But not as we know them. Both require modifications before being applied to the banking sector.

→ The way the market method is used in financial services is to focus on two principal multiples, rather than the raft of earnings multiples we're used to.

$\rightarrow$ Banking and insurance companies have a whole different set of value drivers that need to be understood in order to value them correctly.

FURTHER READING

Jean Dermine, *Bank Valuation and Value-Based Management*, McGraw-Hill, New York, 2009.

Justin J. Camp, *Venture Capital Due Diligence*, John Wiley & Sons, New York, 2002.

Victor Rudenno, *The Mining Valuation Handbook*, John Wiley & Sons, Sydney, 2009.

Jeffrey C. Hooke, *Security Analysis and Business Valuation on Wall Street*, John Wiley & Sons, Hoboken, 2010.

Part II

How do I assess risks to value?

Chapter 6

How green are your assumptions?

What you risk reveals what you value.
— Jeanette Winterson, *The Passion*

If you google 'Archie Karas', the descriptions 'greatest gambler' and 'biggest loser' will both pop up on your screen. Archie Karas, it seems, was both. The poverty-stricken Greek immigrant ran away from home at just 15 years of age, heading to the USA to make his fortune. What a fortune it was. Karas arrived in Las Vegas in 1992 with US$50 to his name and a penchant for card games; over the next six months, in the longest and largest recorded hot streak in history, Karas turned his lousy US$50 into US$17 million in cold, hard cash. Not bad for his first visit to Sin City. The *New York Post* reported: 'He built that into US$40 million and then hit a bad streak and lost US$30 million in three weeks and the other US$10 million in record time as well'.[28] Journalist Linda Stasi commented, 'They say you never knew if Archie would be chauffeured around in a Benz or sleeping in one'.[29]

It's fitting to start with Archie Karas because this chapter is all about streaks — both in corporate bets and in gambling. Unfortunately, though, it's not a 'how to' guide for creating your own streaks like Archie's. Instead, it concentrates on how to ignore the streaks you've had in the past and focus on the game that you're playing right now.

Naturally, we all expect that whenever we're enjoying a winning streak — in any form — it will last forever. We're all very good at overinflating our chances of success, based on any success we've had in the past. But games aren't like that: how you did yesterday (if a game is fair) is often just a matter of luck. Moreover, how you fare tomorrow is simply a matter of how the game is structured. It has nothing to do with any perceived streak. But before we get into how naïve, or green, our valuation assumptions can be, let's look at what Part II of this book is all about.

Risks to value

This second section is dedicated to risk. Having explored the five steps to assessing value in the previous section, Part II covers the various ways we can look at and manage risk. Each chapter in this section builds on the last to enhance your understanding of risk. As the Archie Karas example suggests, there are also plenty of gambling analogies on the cards for this second section. The risks inherent in gambling are not unlike the risks inherent in business valuation and the art in both lies in managing that risk. In fact, the mathematical field of probability originated from the study of games of chance and gambling back in the 16th century.

Gambling as a game of probability fascinates me. When I was only five years old my dad placed a bet for me on the Melbourne Cup. Like any five-year-old punter I made my selection based solely on the horse's name. Back in 1974 I liked the idea of 'Think Big' so I put my 50 cents on that horse and couldn't believe my luck when it romped home. In fact, it won the following year too, so by then I fancied myself as a bit of a gun punter. I can credit my long-standing interest in probability, which started there, as one of the main reasons I chose valuation as a career. The similarities between the two really are that great.

To kick things off, Chapter 6 examines the first big risk in valuation (and one found in Archie Karas's winning — and losing — streaks): being too optimistic with your base line. It reveals the tiny, single-cell formula that can trip up entire baseline valuations. It also explores the common mathematical behaviour of all valuation ratios and how you can use this knowledge to work out the long-term sustainable profitability of your business.

The next chapter explores what a change in your assumptions — no matter how small — can mean for your level of insight. Chapter 7 asks: How sensitive are your valuation assumptions? Or just how wrong can you be?

In Chapter 8 the focus turns outwards. The external environment is not ever fully random, and therefore sets of scenarios (such as an industry price war) exist that impact all of our assumptions.

Chapter 9 brings together the material covered in Chapter 7 (sensitivities) and Chapter 8 (scenarios) to give a range of outcomes.

Finally, the emerging field of prediction markets is explored in Chapter 10. These markets provide a lot of information, not just about the expectation of future events but also about the range of variability around them.

Graphically, Part II looks like a series of building blocks as each chapter adds to the previous:

Figure 21: 5 steps to understanding and managing risk

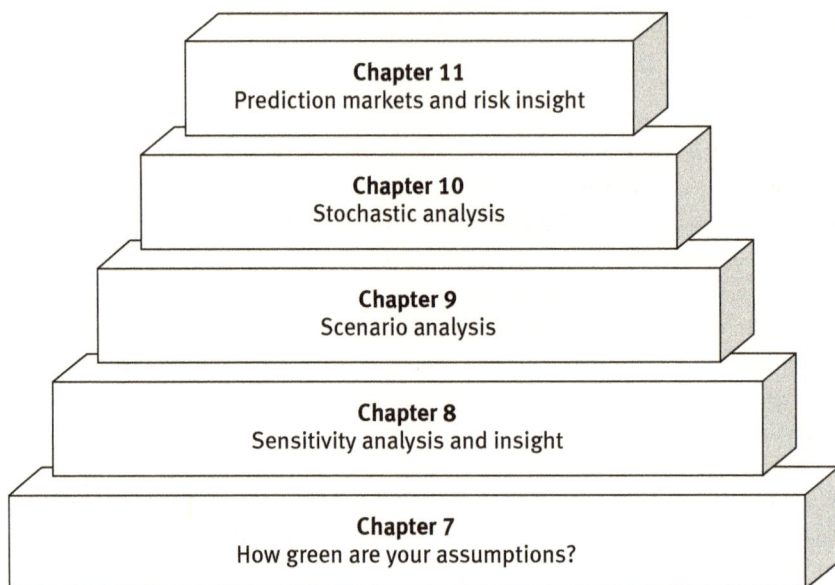

Chapter 11
Prediction markets and risk insight

Chapter 10
Stochastic analysis

Chapter 9
Scenario analysis

Chapter 8
Sensitivity analysis and insight

Chapter 7
How green are your assumptions?

How green are your assumptions?

When it comes to valuation, there's no one right answer. Just as you can occasionally beat the house off the back of a bad bet — simply through sheer luck — it is possible to survive poor business valuation decisions. What valuation offers, however, is the opportunity to make sure you pay the right price for a bet so that over the long term you win.

Taking this principle from the card room to the board room means that it is possible to pay more for an acquisition than it's worth and occasionally get away with it; however, the chances of this happening reduce the more you pay over the 'right' value. Essentially, you're less likely to succeed in the long run if your valuations are repeatedly incorrect.

So how do you ensure your valuations are accurate? Let's start by looking at the biggest risk to any valuation: overestimating your baseline assumptions. This can put you behind the eight ball from the start.

Key value drivers

To make sure you're not too optimistic in your baseline assumptions, we need to turn to the valuation framework. Chapter 3 examined the way a DCF works mechanically and we discovered that a small error in any one of the individual drivers can multiply out to produce a very large error in the total. Now I'm going to equip you with ways to minimise the chances of that happening.

By way of reminder, the critical drivers we focused on in earlier chapters (for industrial companies) were:

→ revenue growth
→ profit margins
→ tax rates
→ capital investment (including working capital and fixed assets, or property, plant and equipment)
→ the cost of capital.

But there is one more critical assumption to consider: the terminal growth rate. The terminal growth rate reflects the ongoing growth potential of your cash flows. In a large valuation model, the terminal growth rate is only one tiny formula that occupies one small cell in your spreadsheet. But don't be fooled. The terminal growth rate is an exponential factor, so it has a massive impact on value. Despite being easily overlooked, it is a major assumption in your calculation, and most valuations, even if they're carried out reasonably in the short term, can prove badly wrong over time if the terminal growth rate is wide of the mark.

Estimation errors

Each of the value drivers outlined above — including the terminal growth rate — can have a dramatic impact on value. Moreover, each is subject to a range of estimation errors. The most common of these include:

→ if growth rate is above the market average, many people expect to sustain this over a long period of time
→ if margins are high, many expect them to continually improve
→ if capital efficiency is high, many believe no competitor is ever going to do any better.

All of these are unlikely to be correct. The reason they're unlikely comes down to two factors.

1. Law of large numbers

As your company grows in size the percentage differences in growth become harder to achieve. This is described colloquially as the 'law of large numbers'.[30]

Take PwC as an example. BRW's Top 100 Accounting Firms list for 2006 placed PwC at number one with an annual revenue (fees) of $1,104,000,000.[31] For PwC to grow at, say, 5 per cent would require an upswing of $55,200,000. That is, we would need to grow by more than the entire size of Ferrier Hodgson, which was ranked at number 18 on the BRW list and is not an insignificant firm.[32] Clearly it's much harder for PwC as a large company to grow at 5 per cent because of our size. A smaller firm could achieve 5 per cent growth more easily.

2. Competition

In a competitive marketplace, it's unlikely you're going to get away with outperforming the market for long, unless you possess a hard-to-copy advantage like scale economies. Why? Because if you're winning, your competitors will simply emulate what you're doing.

Value driver ratios

So now we know what our value drivers are not likely to do, let's look at what assumptions we can make about them. The George O. May Professor of Accounting at Columbia University, Stephen Penman, has some important things to say about the behaviour of value driver ratios over time. Penman studied various US companies over a prolonged period to understand how various ratios performed; the results were intriguing.

What Penman found was that sales growth rates across the market tend to converge around the mean. Penman explains in his book *Financial Statement Analysis and Security Valuation* that 'sales growth tends to fade quickly: firms with high sales growth currently (in the upper groups) have lower sales growth subsequently; firms with low current sales growth (in the lower group) have higher sales growth subsequently'.[33] So estimating a high level of sales growth based on the fact that this was what you achieved last year could potentially prove very misleading.

Driver patterns for sales growth rates are shown by Penman to look like this:

Figure 22: Sales growth rates[34]

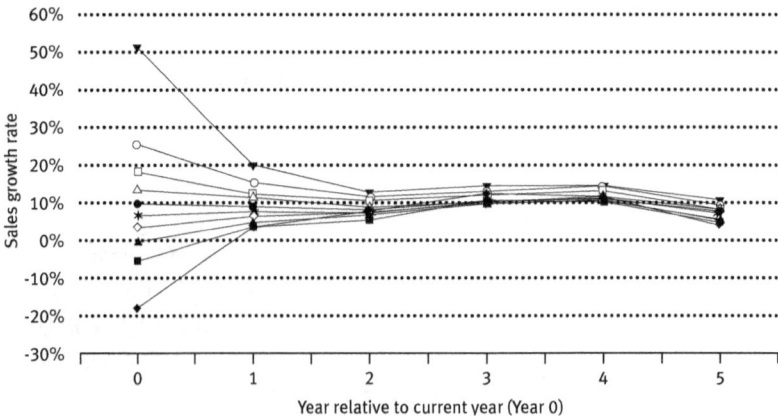

As for core sales profit margins, Penman tells us any changes in these ratios disappear as businesses trend towards common levels close to zero.[35] That is, they behave exactly the same as sales growth figures tend to: they head towards the market mean. Interestingly, those companies that are underperforming in terms of profit often manage to fix their profit woes and even pull ahead of the market for a few years (as shown in the graph below). Here, those at the bottom end are simply catching up with the rest of the market. According to Penman, changes in core sales profit margins across the board look like this:

Figure 23: Changes in core sales profit margins[36]

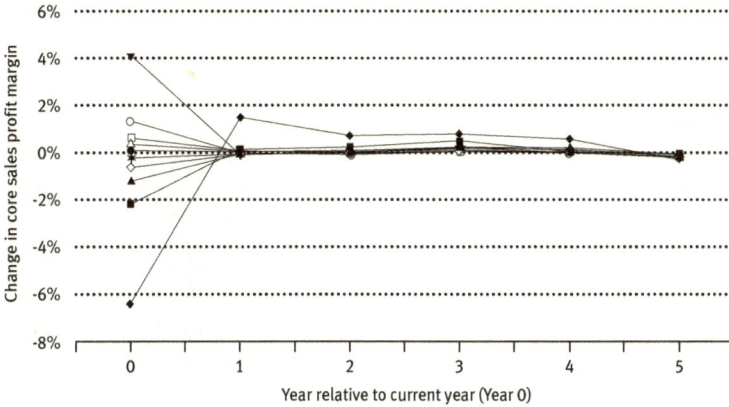

And what about the level of capital intensity, as measured by asset turnover (ATO)? You guessed it. Asset turnover levels also revert towards common levels, and any significant increase or decrease in ATO outside of the norm is usually only temporary.

Figure 24: Changes in asset turnovers[37]

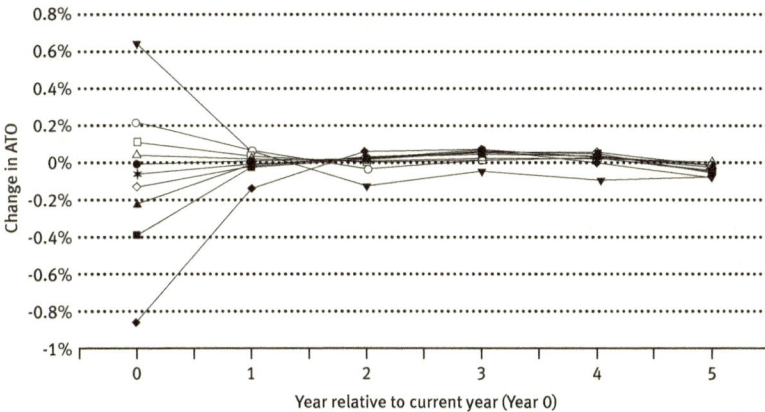

Penman shows us that all of the value drivers we've talked about exhibit this same phenomenon; they all converge on one common market level. Even companies that have previously performed badly tend to stabilise, and this is evident in almost any ratio.

The mathematical behaviour on display is called mean reversion (which we looked at in Chapter 2) and can be put down to the two factors just outlined: the law of large numbers and competition. Most important, however, is what this means for our valuation estimations: your results can return to the mean very quickly. So when forecasting you need to dedicate a lot of time to working out what the long-term sustainable profitability of your business is and that, in turn, determines where each of these ratios lies. Any time your forecasted results are significantly higher or lower than the market mean, you might want to double-check your valuation.

Cost of capital

The other variable worth considering is the cost of capital. With large companies, such as ASX 200 or overseas equivalents, there are only limited variations to the cost of capital. As companies get smaller, however, there are other factors that come into play and can affect the cost of capital. These factors are things like size premiums, which reflect that smaller companies are more risky and more likely to fail than their larger counterparts. The cost of capital is generally considered to be a very sensitive factor and, as it's highly sensitive, large errors can occur.

> When it comes to the cost of equity capital, there are two main factors that are variable. One is the market risk premium (which is the factor that the beta gets multiplied by) and the other is the beta itself.

When it comes to the cost of equity capital, there are two main factors that are variable. One is the market risk premium (which is the factor that the beta gets multiplied by) and the other is the beta itself.

Market risk premium

Market risk premium is commonly believed to be a long-term measure that stands unchanged at 6 per cent in Australia. While this is certainly the convention, you can't just take it as given and should be aware of the current market situation before putting a figure on market risk premium. In reality, this figure ebbs and flows just like every market premium.

Beta factors

The second risk element is beta factors. Beta estimates the degree to which your individual stock contributes to the riskiness of the market as a whole. Essentially, it says that when you buy stock you only get compensated for what it adds to the whole risk of the market; this is what beta is intended to capture. It also measures the co-variance of your stock with the broader market. In other words, how closely does your stock track the vicissitudes of the market?

It's not uncommon for there to be a lot of estimation error around the beta factor due to the high degree of judgement involved. My advice? When determining the beta factor for your business, your best bet is to consider both industry averages and your stock's historical beta. As always, in valuation you need to apply judgement, not just robotic analysis.

Terminal growth rate

The final factor is the terminal growth rate that we talked about earlier in the chapter. Because of its high sensitivity, this is often a very difficult assumption. However, there are two factors that come up in valuations all the time, and once you know what to look out for, these two factors can make estimating the terminal growth rate easier:

1. Determining the terminal period

One of the main decisions in calculating your terminal growth rate is choosing the point at which you think the business has exited the growth phase and become mature. Say you're looking at a company that has a very high competitive advantage from the outset; if you allow, say, five years, they will still have much of that competitive advantage built into their profitability. As this erodes over time, their profits will decline accordingly.

In this situation the onus of proof should be for the valuer to justify why the terminal value should feature growth or returns in excess of long-run industry averages.

If you start your terminal year too early and you haven't yet reached that normal year of profitability (or the long-term competitive equilibrium of that industry), then you're probably over-valuing your business in the zone shown in the graph below.

Figure 25: Calculating the terminal growth rate

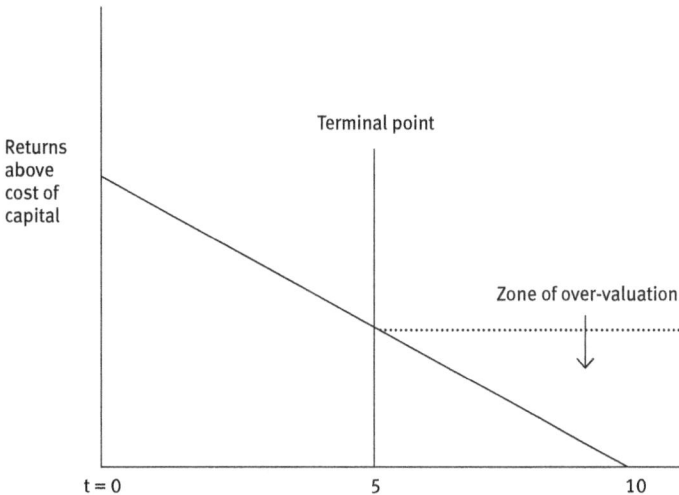

2. Factoring in too much growth

Conventionally, many valuers use inflation growth to work out the terminal growth rate. What this means is that cash flows in perpetuity are expected to stay the same in real terms as the cash flows. Use any more than that and you're effectively saying your returns on capital will continue to increase over time (and we now know they don't), and eventually your business will outgrow the economy in which it resides. So if you use any more than inflation as your factor here, you're probably overestimating your returns.

KEY TAKEAWAYS

→ While it won't always guarantee you bet right each time, valuation does ensure you pay the right price for a corporate bet. So over the long term you win.

→ Often the biggest risk to the accuracy of your valuation is overestimating your baseline assumptions.

→ Each of the value drivers outlined — including the terminal growth rate — can have a dramatic impact on value. Moreover, each is subject to a range of estimation errors.

→ For all the main drivers, your forecast error is likely to be large if you assume much greater than your current performance.

FURTHER READING

Stephen Penman, *Financial Statement Analysis and Security Valuation*, McGraw-Hill, New York, 2009.

Tim Ogier, John Rugman and Lucinda Spicer, *The Real Cost of Capital: A Business Field Guide to Better Financial Decisions*, Pearson, London, 2004.

Chapter 7

Sensitivity analysis and insights

Something as small as the flutter of a butterfly's wing can ultimately cause a typhoon halfway around the world.
— Chaos theory

What weighs 200 kilograms, is 61 metres long and 417 metres high? The answer is a piece of wire. But no ordinary wire. Incredibly, on a warm summer's day back in 1975, these were the measurements of the cable on which French high-wire artist, Philippe Petit, performed his death-defying dance between the Twin Towers in New York. From the time Petit stepped off the Southern Tower and on to his steel cable, chiacking and cavorting and, at one stage, even lying down on the wire, he performed no fewer than eight crossings between the towers. The whole time, those 200 kilograms of cable were all that stood between the daredevil and certain death.

When interviewed about his high-wire party trick, Petit talked about 'the song of my cable':

> *When I walk on the wire the song ... is not heard, but a poet will hear it. Or a five years [sic] old kid who's sensitive will see it, there is an accord, there is a music that is not an imposed song from the wire walker, certainly not an imposed song from the cable but ... everything is perfect. Then there is a song of communion.*[38]

But what if Petit's cable was just a little off key that day? What if, with just one minuscule step to the left or right, or just one unexpected gust of wind, Petit and his cable were singing a song of a very different tune?

This kind of thinking is analogous to sensitivity analysis, because sensitivity analysis is all about 'what if?' What if I make a small change to my forecasts for the business? Will the impact be much more than small? In the words of chaos theory, could a small adjustment to the flapping of a butterfly's wings at this point cause a typhoon for the business further down the track? It's worth remembering the story of Philippe Petit and his high-wire act when we're looking at sensitivity analysis in order to fully appreciate the impact a small change can have.

Sensitivity analysis: an example

The example we run through here is a real-life example in every sense: calculating the cost of running a car. Firstly, it's a situation that most people will come across at some point in their lives. But more than that, this is an actual project I was asked to undertake in my role as a corporate value advisory specialist with PwC. When asked to work out how best to influence and reduce the costs of running a client's car fleet, my colleagues and I came up with the following spreadsheet. This spreadsheet can be just as easily used to calculate the cost of what's in your garage at home and how long you should hold it for.

Figure 26: Assumptions for the cost of running a car (based on a medium-sized car)

Costs of running a car	
Petrol	2250
Maintenance	500
Registration	500
Insurance	1000
Tyres	200
Depreciation	6000
Total	10450
Annual kilometres	15000

Figure 27: Sensitivities for the cost of running a car

Annual kilometres					
Holding period (years) $0.70	5,000	10,000	5,000	20,000	25,000
1	$2.00	$1.10	$0.80	$0.65	$0.56
2	$1.70	$0.95	$0.70	$0.57	$0.50
3	$1.50	$0.85	$0.63	$0.52	$0.46
4	$1.35	$0.77	$0.58	$0.49	$0.43

To arrive at this spreadsheet we factored in all the costs associated with running a car, such as petrol, maintenance, registration and insurance, and then ran a sensitivity analysis. This allowed us to see what happens if we change each variable by the same amount. For instance, we looked at the impact it would have if we change all the factors listed here by 5 or 10 per cent.

The main sensitivities we tested for were driving distance and years of holding. Essentially, we asked: What effect do annual driving distance and holding period have on the cost of running a car? This is calculated in terms of the total cost of the car versus how long you should hold it for. As you can see from the spreadsheet, the more kilometres you do in a year, the more the per-kilometre costs of running your car decrease (from a starting point of $0.70). This is because petrol costs, as well as things like wear and tear on your tyres, general maintenance and so on, do increase by the kilometres travelled but many more costs remain fixed and get spread over more kilometres. Plus, if you hold on to your car for longer, the costs begin to decrease due to depreciation, levelling off after very steep early years.

Why do a sensitivity analysis?

The main reason for carrying out a sensitivity analysis is to identify the key factors that should drive your decision making for a particular aspect of your business. Generally, we test what a 5 or 10 per cent variation in all related factors will do to your final result and then make arbitrary changes based on the impact observed.

Sticking with our car example above, a sensitivity analysis would test what happens if we change all of the factors listed by a certain amount in order to identify the single major factor involved in running a car; this is where sensitivity analysis can get interesting. It turns out the biggest impact to the cost of running a car is not fuel, as most people would expect; in fact, petrol only accounts for between 20 and 25 per cent of the cost of running a car. Instead, the major contributing factor is depreciation, which contributes a whopping 50 per cent of total costs. Accordingly, a 10 per cent increase in depreciation would blow a 10 per cent increase in fuel costs out of the water, as our analysis shows.

Sensitivity analysis, therefore, is invaluable for spelling out exactly which factors you need to understand and focus on within your business. It gives a much finer appreciation of what drivers you should look at in detail, as well as which ones you should look at first. For instance, if it were vitally important for you to get the cost/km right on your company's car fleet you would want to know two things for certain:

→   What's the depreciation charge going to be?
→   What is likely to be the average number of kilometres travelled?

This sort of analysis also ensures it's very easy to defend your conclusions to others by making it simple to explain why your answer is at least reasonable. We often do this within a business valuation by putting ranges of some of the key drivers around any desired result. For example, say we were required to keep our results within $0.10 of $0.70 per kilometre travelled. Even if we changed all the factors in our 'Cost of running a car' spreadsheet by 10 per cent, this still offers a range of outcomes for staying within our required parameters. These outcomes are highlighted in Figure 26.

> Sensitivity analysis can often reveal problems that a more complex model wouldn't show.

You could actually be quite wrong in your decision-making and still get relatively close to your desired result. In this case, you could hold onto your vehicle for anywhere between one and four years and do anywhere between 10,000 and 25,000 kilometres and still be within $0.10 of $0.70. Here $0.70 doesn't look like a bad estimate.

Also, and despite being a really simple of method of analysis, sensitivity analysis can often reveal problems that a more complex model wouldn't show. For instance, it provides you with an opportunity to refine your valuation model based on your results. Returning to our car example again, I've modelled depreciation here on the basis of a certain standard amount or rate of depreciation every year, but if you've ever owned a car you'll know it's not just the age of the car that affects depreciation, but also the number of kilometres driven and how well maintained the vehicle is. All of these things suddenly become very important when you discover — through our spreadsheet — that depreciation is the major factor affecting the cost of your car.

As you can see, sensitivity analysis offers high-value information. It's really fast to do, really cheap to do and there are a range of spreadsheet tools available to make it even easier and cheaper. Ideally, it is something you should carry out during every valuation exercise. The important thing to note is when to do it.

When to carry out sensitivity analysis

When working on an assignment or project where value is important, my advice is to put together a quick model and then run a sensitivity analysis that indicates where you should spend your time when creating a more detailed model. In a business context, if a sensitivity analysis shows that my margin is of greatest importance then I should spend all my time understanding what it is that drives my margin and not focus too heavily on other factors like growth. Carrying out a sensitivity analysis early in the process to identify your key factor/s is a very useful thing to do — rather than doing it at the end of the process and finding out you were focused on the wrong driver throughout. In fact, the best option is to do more than one sensitivity analysis for any one project so that it acts as a feedback loop throughout the process.

> As you can see, sensitivity analysis offers high-value information. It's really fast to do, really cheap to do and there are a range of spreadsheet tools available to make it even easier and even cheaper to run.

As a final note on sensitivity analysis, and to highlight the diverse application of the model, let's apply it briefly to the concept of a carbon tax. As I write, debate is still raging over how much or little difference a carbon tax would make, and how much or little water levels would have to rise to have a meaningful impact. At the Powerhouse Museum in Sydney recently, my son and I observed an image of what Sydney would look like after just a one-metre rise in water levels. (Most of Circular Quay, the main ferry terminal in Sydney, was flooded.) This shows another way of looking at sensitivity analysis — in this case, the sensitivity of Sydney to just one metre of water. Right now, no-one knows whether current carbon dioxide levels are capable of raising sea levels by one metre, but sensitivity analysis asks the question: Should you care? If you own property around Circular Quay, it seems you really should.

KEY TAKEAWAYS

→ Sensitivity analysis is invaluable for identifying exactly which key factors you need to understand and focus on.

→ It's also useful for defending your conclusions and explaining why your result/s are at least reasonable.

→ Essentially, sensitivity analysis is a simple but powerful tool that should be applied at multiple stages throughout the valuation process.

Chapter 8

Scenario analysis: the world through different lenses

There are known knowns; there are things we know we know.
We also know there are known unknowns; that is to say we
know there are some things we do not know. But there are
also unknown unknowns — there are things we don't know
we don't know. — Donald Rumsfeld, US politician

In the 2008 box-office smash hit film *21* viewers meet Ben Campbell, an MIT senior math major, who finds himself inadvertently joining the school black-jack team and learning the fine art of card counting. As Campbell tells viewers: 'I had a 1590 on my SAT, I got a 44 on my MCAT, and I have a 4.0 GPA from MIT. I thought I had my life mapped out, but then I remembered what my non-linear equations professor once told me: always account for variable change ...' Because this is Hollywood, variable change comes in the form of 17 trips to Vegas, hundreds of thousands of dollars being won, hundreds of thousands of dollars being stolen and, of course, an old school romance.

What's interesting is that *21* is inspired by the true story of the MIT black-jack team. What's more interesting is that the movie provides us with a good example of scenario analysis. In *21* the blackjack team successfully uses a whole bunch of modelling techniques to calculate the best time to place their bets. That is, they use card counting. Card counting works a little like scenario analysis in that players use the information available to them to classify their game as one of several possible betting scenarios. When a number of cards have been played, it changes the odds of what's left in the pack and, when a certain number of cards play out, or when certain individual cards play out, there's a set number of scenarios that can take place.

For instance, when all the high cards in a pack come out early, there are clearly more low cards left and a bust for the dealer is less likely. Here, you bet less and you bet low because this scenario has changed the odds against you. All blackjack players have two basic scenarios: a hot pack and a cold pack. A hot pack simply means there are plenty of high cards left in the pack (as I've just described), whereas a cold pack is when there are more low cards remaining and a lesser risk of the dealer going bust.

When should I use scenario analysis?

In a corporate environment, however, there are many more than two basic scenarios, so you would expect scenario analysis to enjoy a more central role here than it does in blackjack, right? Wrong. One of the key issues with scenario analysis is that so often people carry out their analysis after their valuation is complete.

Many of us concentrate on our base estimate exclusively (that is, everything we've covered in Chapters 1–5), making scenario analysis (and also sensitivity analysis) simply an afterthought. There is a tendency to spend all our time coming up with a valuation figure, using the information we already know about the business (or the 'known knowns' as Rumsfeld so inarticulately put it), rather than putting our energies into assessing risk (or the 'known unknowns'). This is not the way it should be. Scenario analysis should be integrated into our valuation analysis so that, rather than focus on how right we are, we look at how wrong we can be. This is the crux of valuation.

What is scenario analysis?

Scenario analysis is all about choosing different futures. Where sensitivity analysis says 'This is one view of the future' (and if that view is wrong, how great is the difference?), scenario analysis looks at a range of combinations of possible circumstances and asks: 'How does that range affect the total?'

Sensitivity analysis is often demonstrated using a typical valuation model. Rather than do this, and choose an example or industry that may be more relevant to some readers than others, I apply sensitivity analysis to an everyday example that we can all relate to. This way, we can spend our time concentrating on the analysis itself and not, perhaps, struggling with the relevance of the example. We do, however, visit a high-end example later in the chapter when we look at the use of stress testing by major banks.

For now, let's consider one basic scenario that most of us will have experienced: the purchase of a car. I've used the spreadsheet from Chapter 7 to generate this scenario. Throughout this example, I use exactly the same techniques I would apply for a sensitivity analysis in a corporate context, only here it becomes obvious more quickly where we should invest our time and energy.

Let's say you have a choice of a small, medium or large car. In making this decision, what are the different possible scenarios to consider?

This example has been worked out in the spreadsheet here.

Figure 28: Assumed costs of running a car

Car type	Medium	Small	Large
Petrol	2,250	1,800	3,375
Maintenance	500	500	500
Rego	500	500	500
Insurance	1,000	1,000	1,000
Tyres	200	200	200
Depreciation	5,000	3,333	6,333
	9,450	7,333	11,909
Annual kilometres	15,000	15,000	15,000

Figure 29: Scenario analysis by cost per kilometre

Residual values	Medium	Small	Large
1 year	75%	80%	70%
2 years	60%	65%	60%
3 years	50%	60%	50%
4 years	43%	50%	40%
Holding period	3	3	3

	Medium	Small	Large
Cost per kilometre	$0.63	$0.49	$0.79
Economy	10	8	15
Fuel costs	1.5	1.5	1.5
New cost	$30,000	$25,000	$38,000

The scenario analysis shows us that the small car costs less, has slightly less depreciation per annum (because there's less value overall) and is more economical to run. By way of contrast, the large car costs more, its depreciation curve is sharper and it uses a lot more fuel. Running these figures through a scenario analysis shows us that, in this example, it costs you significantly more to own a large car than a small car.

But this is intuitive. Why do I need a scenario analysis to tell me a small car will be cheaper to run than a larger car? Also, what's the difference between a sensitivity analysis and scenario analysis?

Sensitivity analysis versus scenario analysis

The major difference between the sensitivity and scenario methods of analysis is their scope. In sensitivity analysis you test some arbitrary change in one variable (say, a change of 10 per cent), whereas scenario analysis allows you to examine a whole suite of circumstances that could change. Circumstances like switching to a different sized car.

Plus, thinking in terms of scenarios helps us to think beyond the artificiality of a sensitivity analysis. Where sensitivity analysis can be overtly simple in a way that doesn't accurately reflect reality, scenario analysis lets us build in different futures — which may or may not be equally likely — in order to ask: If X happened, what would I do?

The main benefit of sensitivity analysis is that it tells us much about the value of information, whereas the main benefit of scenario analysis is that it tells us what actions we should take in response to that information. As you can see, the two analyses work well together as they complement one another.

Stress testing

Scenario analysis is often used by banks and other financial institutions, where it's called stress testing (a term that has become particularly popular post-GFC). What typically happens is that a bank or financial institution will examine situations that have occurred in the past and ask: What happens if we go through this again? The organisation in question doesn't know how likely it is that these significant events from the past will be repeated; the point here is to test whether the bank would survive if they did. So a bank might ask itself: What happens if we have a crash equivalent to September 11? Or another Black Monday circa 1987? Or a repeat of the 1929 Great Depression? If a similar percentage change were to occur, what would that do to our capital position? If a bank's stress tests on these scenarios come out positive, they earn the approval of their regulator. If negative, they need more capital.

The scenarios tested in stress testing are never small variations from the normal; they're large and damaging hypothetical situations. The scenarios tested may also differ wildly from one another, depending on what you're testing. Banks generally implement a whole range of scenarios because they have particularly complicated value models that describe how the business is performing. Banks often rely on measurements like price changes from day to day — where they assume a normal distribution — to assess performance.[39] Of course, price changes are not normally distributed but it's a convenient fiction for banks to use to describe what happens from day to day.

The problem here is that these normal distributions don't explain what happens during exceptional circumstances, such as the crash of 1987, so this is where scenario stress tests come in. Scenarios are imperative when you're looking at strategic cases or strategic situations where a whole range of factors move in directions you can't anticipate.

Moreover, banks and financial institutions assume some correlation. A great example in financial markets is the assumption that, when interest rates fall, the value of the stock market goes up. Also, when share markets head south, the price of gold heads north. These are only a couple of many commonly assumed relationships that are taken to be related.

But it's differences in correlation that offer some form of insurance. Say you had two events that weren't correlated, such as two hands of blackjack. If you play two hands at one time, you effectively reduce your chances of losing both hands. You might have a 50/50 chance of winning one hand and a 50/50 chance of winning the other, but you're far less likely to lose both than you are to just lose one. Roughly half as likely, in fact. Why? Because you're diversifying your risk.

Which is fine except during periods of great stress. During financial crises, instead of no correlation, things suddenly start to become highly correlated. For instance, in 2008 the price of equity (which was generally assumed to be highly disassociated in terms of market performances) changed rapidly to a position of perfect correlation, causing everything to fall at once. Bankers worldwide were playing two hands of blackjack when all the diversity they were banking on disappeared overnight. The bottom line? Our nice mathematical models of normal distribution and correlation can fail when the chips are down.

To mitigate against this, we need to put into place scenario analyses that not only assume that a once-in-a-lifetime event such as The Great Depression is just around the corner, but that also assume our everyday correlations all suddenly become perfectly correlated. Now how does your business look? Can you survive that?

The answer is probably not.

That's a pretty bleak scenario we've just outlined but a valuable one nonetheless, because the answers to those questions give you some idea of how resilient your business is. That's where the value of scenario analysis lies. It puts the critical questions to businesses: If a certain disaster scenario happened, what would you do? How would you survive? What actions would you need to take? This way you can develop your contingency plan accordingly.

KEY TAKEAWAYS

→ Business valuation is all about how wrong we could be, rather than how right we are. Accordingly, scenario analysis should be integrated into our valuation analysis rather than considered as an afterthought.

→ Sensitivity analysis and scenario analysis are highly complementary. Sensitivity analysis tells us much about the value of information and scenario analysis tells us what actions we should take in response to that information.

→ Scenario analysis tests our business's resilience in large and damaging situations.

Chapter 9

Stochastic analysis: a trip to Monaco

*If you ain't just a little scared when you enter a casino, you
are either very rich or your haven't studied the games enough.*
— VP Pappy, famous poker player

In the 1940s, at the height of World War II, the Allied forces' most brilliant
analytical minds were assembled in Los Alamos Scientific Laboratory in the
Chihuahuan Desert, Albuquerque. Their mission? To develop nuclear weapons.
This was on the advice — from Albert Einstein, no less — that Germany was
doing likewise. While these brain boxes of the Manhattan Project (as it became
known) had access to the most advanced scientific data available at the time, the
group had to stop short of coming up with a definitive mathematical solution.
Desert or not, there's not a lot of scope for testing your hypothesis when you're
working in nuclear physics.

Instead, the Manhattan Project invented methods of simulation that relied
on repeated random sampling to calculate their results. This technique was
dubbed the Monte Carlo analysis. The name was coined by mathematicians
John von Neumann and Stanislaw Ulam, and paid homage to the famed Monte
Carlo casino where Ulam's uncle regularly gambled. Not only was a code name
necessary for security purposes, it was also much catchier than 'computational
algorithms in the form of stochastic analysis'.

The Manhattan Project represented possibly the greatest collection of geni-
uses ever gathered together in one place in the history of humankind. In terms
of intellectual achievement over a short period of time, it stands alone. Ever
since then, stochastic analysis has been known as Monte Carlo analysis and this
technique has proven invaluable — not just to nuclear physics but to business
as well.

Monte Carlo analysis

Monte Carlo analysis is a method of simulation that relies on repeated random sampling. It combines sensitivity analysis (see Chapter 7) and scenario analysis (see Chapter 8) but adds a little twist, not unlike a cocktail. You see, the Monte Carlo technique builds on what we've learned about conducting sensitivity and scenario analyses by assessing the probabilities of selected outcomes occurring, effectively taking sensitivity and scenario analyses one step further. So the twist, if you like, is the added information we get about the probability of the scenarios in question.

The process for carrying out Monte Carlo analysis is twofold. First, we need to gather our inputs, looking at the range in variability that can exist around each input. Next, we sample from that range many, many times. For instance, in the case study we're about to run through I sampled 10,000 times — but you can put your dice away because, thankfully, there are computer programs available that will do this sampling for you. (Unlike the South African physicist back in 1940 who sat down and rolled a dice 10,000 painstaking times by hand.)

Case study

To illustrate stochastic analysis in practice, let's take our example of the car from the previous chapters, where we discovered it cost $0.70 per kilometre to run a medium-sized car. Here, let's ask what the ranges for this car might be — because if I work in finance (and in many other industries too, for that matter), I care not just about averages but also about distributions. Remember we agreed that the costs of running a car are maintenance, tyres, depreciation, petrol, registration and insurance.

Let's start by considering maintenance. In most cases this will cost you little or nothing, assuming we're talking about a brand new car. Unless of course you get a lemon. It's not very often your new car will prove a dud but it can happen, so I've entered a distribution that describes the cost of maintenance being nil (or minimal) most of the time but exorbitant in rare situations.

The cost of tyres is a similar story. If you're unlucky enough to have a blow-out, your tyres can suddenly prove expensive. However, usually the cost involved is simply wear and tear over time.

When we consider depreciation on the number of kilometres driven, there's a distribution here too. Most people drive around 15,000 kilometres a year. Some drive many more than this, while others drive fewer, so this spreads our distribution out a little.

As for petrol prices — well, these go up and down according to external forces such as exchange rates (i.e. when exchange rates head south, generally petrol prices head north).

So we take all these distributions and more (insurance, registration and the like) and enter them into whichever software program you opt for. I used @

RISK from Palisade. @RISK then tossed a coin 10,000 times to calculate what the cost per kilometre is for running a car and the results are shown here:

Figure 30: Costs of running a car (per kilometre)

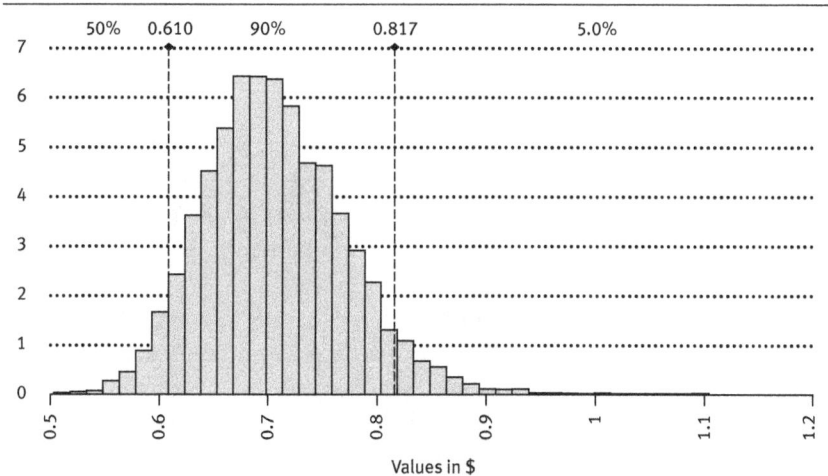

The result for this particular scenario is $0.69 per kilometre (which is very close to the amount of $0.70 we first calculated back in Chapter 7). In addition to this, we learn that the maximum amount your car could cost you per kilometre is $1.10 (and this is only if you travel very few kilometres per year) and the cheapest it could possibly be is $0.50, or about half of the average cost. By way of comparison, the flat rate for your standard taxi is $1.99, not including flag fall and surcharges.

The graph shows there is a significant range between the maximum and minimum cost per kilometre but the extreme cases — $1.10 and $0.50 — are both quite improbable. This distribution of numbers provides us with a sense of just how likely it is that we will be wrong. According to the curve shown, 90 per cent of cases are going to fall between $0.61 and $0.82 and only 5 per cent of cases will be above $0.82.

As you can see, Monte Carlo analysis offers a really good feel for how wide-ranging any one variable can be. If it were really important to you that your car didn't cost you more than $0.80 per kilometre, then you're not running a lot of risk. Or if you can lock your travel costs in at an option, say by choosing to cycle when you know that cycling will cost you $0.52 per kilometre, then by using this Monte Carlo analysis you're able to say that cycling will almost definitely be cheaper.

For a more acute example of the value of Monte Carlo analysis, let's head back to the casino. There is a betting system called Martingale that sounds, on the face of it, unlosable. Under this system, if you toss a coin you double your money every time, so if you bet $1 and flip the coin and win, you put $1 in again. If you lose, however, you double your loss and put $2 in. The expected value of this strategy is zero and anyone betting under the Martingale system can expect to break even, so if you put $1 in up front, you can expect to win that $1 back. The problem with this strategy, however, is that, like any form of gambling, there's risk involved. So if you lose on your $2 bet, you put $4 in. Lose again? Put $8 in. Lose 10 times in a row? Suddenly, where you expected to break even you've lost a lot — and fast.

As the Martingale system shows us, the difference between the expected value ($0.70 per kilometre in the case of our car example) and the actual distribution ($1.10 per kilometre in the worst-case scenario for our car example) can mean that sometimes you'll go very broke, very quickly.

When the normal curve is not normal

The other thing that's evident from this particular example is that the distribution around our travel costs is not even. See how our distribution curve is slightly skewed to the left? During the GFC, a phrase bandied about in financial services was 'value at risk', which is what we see when a normal curve is manipulated. For example, take the Black-Scholes option-pricing model. This model of financial markets uses derivative investment instruments and has, at its heart, a normal distribution of asset values and a lognormal distribution of returns; generally this is not a bad assumption.

Except that there are some things that don't have a normal distribution!

The distribution in our car example, for instance, is slightly skewed to the left. Similarly (as Chapter 8 showed), banks can't apply a normal distribution (without understanding the limitations of that assumption), because their asset prices (or changes in these prices) aren't normally distributed.

So, while the normal curve is a very useful simplification, it's not necessarily an accurate one. It simply doesn't apply in all circumstances, particularly at the fringes of the curve in the so-called 'fail regions'. Although it's fairly unlikely that you're going to get wide variations that can't be described by the standard deviation, unfortunately, market price fluctuations of a certain level do occur and if you only ever believed what a normal curve told you, then disasters like the stock market crash of 1987 simply wouldn't exist. Or at least, not more than once in a lifetime, and certainly not three or four times in the last 20-odd years.

> While the normal curve is a very useful simplification, it's not necessarily an accurate one.

Unfortunately, exceptional circumstances do happen; what's more, they happen every 20 years or so, sometimes less often. It's quite a leap to move from the normal curve's stance of assuming those things very rarely happen, to saying: 'Actually, they happen every 20-odd years.' It tells us that there is something very wrong with those normal distribution assumptions. The question of what exactly is wrong is an area that has been subject to extensive study in recent years, but exploring that area is beyond the scope of this book. Suffice to say here that the beauty of stochastic analysis is, when it is properly used, it recognises the limits of the normal curve and allows us to explore what the range of our risk is.

Risk insight

The corollary of this is that stochastic analysis allows you to determine how much risk you want to take. Using our graph you could say, 'I want just 1 per cent of all cases to sit above my estimate.' In which case you would move your estimated costs outwards, maybe closer to $0.90. This is particularly important when you start thinking about how much debt you can plug into your business, and it's important when you're talking about much bigger figures than $1.00. In our car example, most people wouldn't blink about incurring travel costs that were anywhere between $0.50 and $0.82 per kilometre because it's still cheaper than catching a taxi. But if these were much bigger figures we were talking about, suddenly our decisions become very sensitive to the outcome of our analysis.

Traditionally, it was simply good enough to arrive at our original figure of $0.70 when carrying out a valuation.

Not any more.

Say $0.70 is your target cost and it's really very important to the business that you don't exceed this cost. As the graph above shows, it's almost 50 per cent probable that the cost incurred will be above $0.70, which could mean serious trouble for your bottom line.

In the instance of insurance companies, for example, it's pertinent to ask: How much capital do I need so that my insurance losses don't exceed the amount of money I have, a certain percentage of times? In other words, insurance companies use the exact mode of thinking employed in a stochastic analysis. By looking at the chances of a range of scenarios happening, stochastic analysis allows us to see probability and consequence on the one graph. When you consider that insurance of any form — life, health, home and contents — is certain to cost you a small amount each week but might save you an enormous amount in the future, it's surprising more people don't take out insurance.

On the flipside, the classic case in reverse is lotteries. The payoff of a lottery tells us that most of the time we're going to lose a small amount (through the cost of our lottery ticket) but there's that minuscule percentage of times where someone will win a truckload. Graphically, the distribution of a lottery would look something like this:

Figure 31: Distribution of a lottery

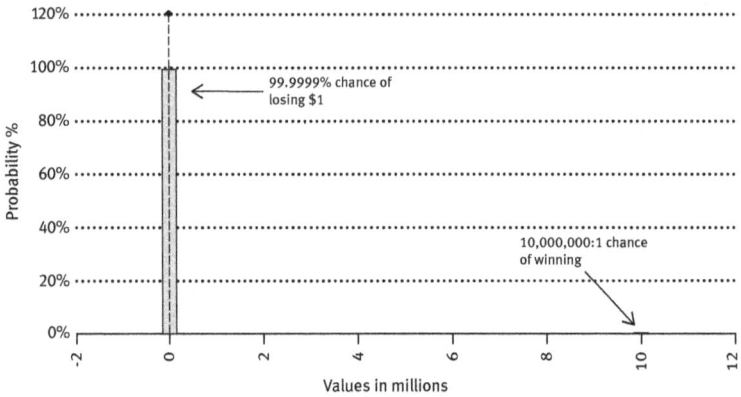

Many people consider this a very favourable distribution, at least favourable enough to pay for the ticket. However, what is most likely to happen is that you'll lose (similarly in insurance contracts). In traditional business valuation, this is almost 'opposite land'; business valuations tend to focus on average outcomes. Yet, as you can see, in gambling and insurance cases, that distribution is an important measure, as well as the average.

The other thing to consider is this: if you could have a car that you knew with absolute certainty was going to cost you $0.70 per kilometre, or a car with the sort of distribution shown in the graph, which one would you prefer? If it were me, I'd choose the former because with the latter, there's a 50 per cent probability that the cost could be more than $0.70. A leasing company, which can diversify the risk involved across many vehicles so can bear the risk, might actually give you an option such as this. (Although, in reality, they'll probably ask for $0.75 per kilometre, charging you a small premium for the certainty.)

> If you had a eureka moment and hit upon an idea that might make you a small fortune, but it was an idea that — nine times out of 10 — would leave you broke, would you do it?

Clearly, stochastic analysis is really useful for understanding the risk involved in any project or investment.

If you had a eureka moment and hit upon an idea that might make you a small fortune, but it was an idea that — nine times out of 10 — would leave you broke, would you do it? Maybe, maybe not. It depends on your tendency for risk aversion. If you were Donald Trump, I'm guessing you'd have a go. But regardless of your risk profile, stochastic analysis enables you to make your judgement fully informed by the facts and, for this reason alone, it's a very useful tool.

But surprisingly, it is not a tool that's often used. Why? Quite simply because it is considerably easier to perform the analyses shown in previous chapters and come up with our initial figure of $0.70 and then go on to do some sensitivity analysis around this and come to the conclusion that most of the time you'll be OK. Of course, most of the time you will. Plus some of the time it just won't matter whether you're OK or not because the outcome won't be that significant. But sometimes you really do care and that's when stochastic analysis is important.

Combining sensitivity, scenario and stochastic analysis

So how do you combine sensitivity, scenario and stochastic analysis? What order should they come in and what role does each play?

Firstly, sensitivity analysis: this mode of analysis is really easy and it's really cheap so there is little excuse for skipping this important step. Depending on the results at this stage, you can choose whether to do a stochastic analysis or not.

For instance, by changing one variable in your sensitivity analysis by 5 per cent, are you altering the outcome by 100 per cent? That sort of result would indicate that your venture or project is highly risky and you probably don't need a stochastic analysis on top to tell you that.

A scenario analysis of the same business might tell you that, most of the time, your business looks OK. It's only in one instance that circumstances may prove a killer, raising the question: How well protected am I? Stress tests should be used accordingly. This is a slightly more sophisticated approach than the first approach outlined above.

However, a stochastic analysis should be used in addition — and used early in the piece. If you understand the distribution for your business, it can prove very valuable for all the reasons outlined earlier in the chapter — not least because it helps you determine how you can fund things.

Monte Carlo analysis is one of the areas where companies are not doing enough. Insurance companies use this method of thinking well — it's their core business, after all. Mining companies tend to be fairly extensive users too. Being highly exposed to metal price and exchange rate fluctuations, mining companies model these (and other parts of the business) as an important part of how they look at diversity across projects. But on the whole, many other companies could benefit by using Monte Carlo analysis, even a little. Most people are just overly optimistic, so the first challenge we face is to stop kidding ourselves about the real risks we face. (The next chapter gives you some tools to help manage that optimism.)

The second challenge is to start asking: How wrong can I be? And on top of this: How unlucky can I be? The techniques outlined in this chapter can help you calculate the probability of that.

KEY TAKEAWAYS

→ Monte Carlo analysis or stochastic analysis combines sensitivity analysis and scenario analysis with the additional benefit of assessing probabilities too.

→ Monte Carlo analysis provides a really good feel for how wide-ranging any one outcome can be.

→ While the normal curve is a useful tool of analysis, it's not always an accurate one; it doesn't apply in all circumstances.

→ The main value of stochastic analysis is that it allows us to see probability and consequence on the one graph.

→ Business valuations often rely on 'average' estimates rather than distributions, meaning that Monte Carlo gives you a much clearer view of how well (or badly) your investment might turn out.

Chapter 10

Prediction markets and risk insights

Prediction is very difficult, especially about the future.
— Neils Bohr, Danish physicist

It's possible, it seems, to bet on almost anything. *Gizmag* online technology magazine reported in January 2010 that last-minute betting on the name of Apple's soon-to-be-released touchscreen tablet had shortened the odds for the leading name — iPad — from 7/4 to 1/3 with Irish bookmaker Paddy Power.[40]

Gizmag went on to explain that, given that the flow of money from the public determines the odds, and that there must be hundreds of thousands of people out there who had been involved in the device's development and who knew its name, they considered iPad to be a sure thing. (They also pointed out that, unlike trading on shares where insider information can land you behind bars, betting sites have few such restrictions.)

Aside from the fact I could never see Steve Jobs signing off some of the other names suggested by Paddy Power (would you buy an iCan, iRead or iBoard?), I agree that *Gizmag's* reasons to back the iPad were sound. Why? Well, if you cast your mind back to Economics 101 you'll remember your lecturer talking about the concept of the efficient market hypothesis. What this hypothesis suggests is that, on the whole, the market is the best (or least biased) predictor of future value. The common consensus is that people can't outperform the sharemarket on average, and that it's virtually impossible to systematically do so over time.

What I've just described to you in our *Gizmag* case study is a prediction market and a great example of how, if you gather an aggregate of opinions, you can actually get an opinion that conveys a lot of information.

Another example of this can be found in James Surowiecki's book *The Wisdom of Crowds*. The book kicks off with an anecdote about a competition to guess the weight of an ox at a country fair. The crowd at the fair accurately guessed the weight of an ox when their individual guesses were averaged. Not only was the crowd's weighted average guess more accurate than any of their individual guesses, it was also closer than any of the separate estimates made by cattle experts that were present, demonstrating the power of the market to predict.

This anecdote, as retold by Surowiecki, comes originally from polymath Francis Galton who, among other things during his lifetime, was responsible for the invention of the statistical concept of correlation, composite photography, the field of behaviour genetics, the phrase 'nature versus nurture', the weather map, the field of differential psychology and the Galton whistle. Would it surprise you to hear he was also the half-cousin of Charles Darwin?

During his spare time, when Galton jotted down the anecdote of the ox, he introduced us to a concept that has been parlayed into the idea of prediction markets and allows us to gauge the probability of certain events happening. Common examples of prediction markets include the ubiquitous Centrebet and Betfair; as I pointed out at the beginning of the chapter, it's now possible to bet on just about anything in Australia, from cricket to cane toad racing, and from federal elections to flies on a wall (well, maybe not flies on a wall).

How prediction markets work

From a valuation point of view, prediction markets work like this. Say the outcome of your business is completely dependent on the results of an upcoming election. You might be in an industry that's highly susceptible to a carbon tax, for instance, and one side of politics (let's say the government) is pushing for a carbon tax while the opposition is against the idea. A prediction market about the election would probably tell you what the value of your exposure would be. Say you work out the impact of a carbon tax on your business, and then you calculate that the probability of the government getting up is 55 per cent. This tells you that the dollar impact of a carbon tax on your business would be 55 per cent of the total exposure. Having an accurate prediction market in such a situation is very useful. That's why it's such a big deal that we can conclude that, under certain circumstances, prediction markets are often superior to any one individual at forecasting the future.

But wait a minute. You'll notice I said that this is only true under certain circumstances. So what are the conditions needed for prediction markets to be accurate?

i) Diversity of opinion: in order for a prediction market to work, each person should have private information, and different private information at that, even if this is simply an eccentric interpretation of the facts.

ii) Independence: people should not be able to copy the next person's views, so that their opinions are not merely determined by the opinions around them.

iii) Decentralisation: people must be able to specialise and bring their own knowledge and information to the table.

iv) Aggregation: mechanisms must exist for turning private judgements into a collective decision. This is what the market does.

These four criteria are usually (but not always) fulfilled by financial markets, so you can confidently use financial markets as a basis for your own predictions. For example, futures prices are as good a predictor as you could ask for. There will always be parameters that must be used in your valuation, so where those parameters exist it's best to stick to the market view. As the above stories relate, the market is usually more accurate anyway, and your choices of parameter will be a lot easier to defend.

Beware the herd mentality

The very idea of prediction markets owes much to Galton's anecdote about oxen, so it's appropriate that I warn you about the herd mentality. For all that prediction markets offer us much in terms of knowledge and information, we do need to be careful about the circumstances in which people can start influencing or believing one another. In other words, beware the herd mentality. This is exactly what played out prior to the GFC; the boom in the mortgage market, especially in the USA, was a typical case of the herd in action. The majority of people believed property prices would continue to rise and acted accordingly, which in turn saw the whole system collapse. While it's all very easy for us to be wise in hindsight, this doesn't change the fact that we should always be aware of herd behaviour of this kind and not just blindly follow the market. So long as you keep in mind that you need to adjust for differences between what you're measuring and the market — say, when you are valuing a controlling interest and the market is pricing minority interests — it's generally safe to assume the market is the very best predictor available. But be aware this doesn't always hold.

DIY prediction markets

As we've discussed, prediction markets exist for a whole range of things and we should always use them where they exist. But what if a prediction market doesn't exist where you need one? You can simply create your own. As long as you have people who are willing to take an independent view, you will always be able to create your own DIY prediction market.

For instance, let's say you have a whole portfolio of R&D proposals and you're wondering about which one to invest in. You can create your own internal portfolio market to predict which is the best idea. Say you have 25 ideas to choose from; simply award value to different shares (you don't have to use real money here, Monopoly money is fine) and then bet on the ones with the highest prices first and cascade the investment down from there. You'll effectively capture all the information that's available to you and you can then use this information to make budgetary decisions. In other words, you have created an internal prediction market.

A number of organisations have successfully done this, including Google, Motorola, Hewlett-Packard, Renault, Eli Lilly, Siemens, Masterfoods, General Electric, MGM and Lionsgate studios, Starwood and Recorded Future. However, the one I really love is the Hollywood Stock Exchange. The Hollywood Stock Exchange is a virtual market game in which participants buy and sell prediction shares of movies, actors, directors and film-related options. This fantastic innovation is regularly used by studios to gauge the potential success of their new movies by allocating a price to each individual movie that's in the production pipeline and then allowing punters to bet on how successful any one movie is going to be in terms of its revenue. Hollywood executives then use this market as a weighted average screen test because, as a prediction market, it is a very effective way of forecasting how much money Hollywood big shots should throw at a movie. In fact, so accurate is the Hollywood Stock Exchange that it correctly predicted 29 of the 37 big-category Oscar nominees in 2009, bringing its 11-year average to 82.1 per cent.

Beyond the market

As you can see, the use of prediction markets is a real growth area and business valuers (and others) are increasingly relying on them. With so many prediction markets around — and the ability to create your own internal market — it really is easier than ever to forecast using an aggregate of opinions. Prediction markets now extend well beyond the hard and fast market to the social network stratosphere.

In his book *Pulse*, US futurist Douglas Hubbard looks at a series of places where there's not so much a market as a sentiment or index of opinion. Places such as Twitter and Facebook. Just as during World War II, when both sides used code breakers to detect key words in enemy translations and then aggregated this information, we can now mine for information quickly and easily using virtual prediction markets like Google, wikis and blogs. Seeing something trending on Google? Noticing a recurring word or theme on Twitter? An aggregate of online opinions is now one of the fastest ways to forecast the future. Hubbard explains how a Canadian epidemiologist is now predicting flu outbreaks faster than the Canadian health authorities, by tracking 'flu symptoms' searches on Google. So successful are his predictions that Google has now established a 'Flu Trends' tool.[41]

In just the same way, people are starting to sit up and take notice of online chatter about short-term changes in the price of securities because it seems such predictions are not a bad basis on which to make investment decisions.

However, the most famous (or infamous) example of using online opinion for prediction was back in 2003, when the US Department of Defense announced a Policy Analysis Market. This was essentially an online trading market where punters could bet on future terrorist attacks, conflicts and assassination attempts — the idea being that online speculation and public opinion was the most accurate means for the Department to predict where the next terrorist attack might occur. Public outcry immediately erupted over the so-called 'terrorism futures market' with Senate Democratic Leader Tom Daschle labelling it 'perhaps the most irresponsible, outrageous and poorly thought out of anything I have heard from this administration'.[42] Needless to say, the website was shut down before it ever got off the ground.

This doesn't take away from the fact that overall, prediction markets (whether they be external, internal or simply a gauge of online sentiment) are an invaluable tool for predicting the future. As a relatively new concept, however, these markets are not regularly used in business valuation. Valuers will comfortably use financial market predictions, but we tend to be less sanguine about other types of prediction markets. This is to our detriment. Economists as a whole are systematically terrible at predicting the future (insert your own economist joke here), so why not look to something that's proven to be a better forecaster?

No money-back guarantee

Before you ask for your free set of steak knives, however, it's worth noting that prediction markets do not guarantee a result; they only give an indication of how probable it is. Put simply, if you bet on a prediction market assuming it's a certainty, you're going to be disappointed. In fact, if you bet on a prediction market that says something is only 50 per cent probable, you're going to be disappointed 50 per cent of the time. While prediction markets provide you with valuable information, they will never give you certainty because, when it comes to the future, there is no such thing as a sure thing. There are, however, new and evolving technologies, particularly in the more uncertain areas of valuation (such as early-stage technology) that can be used to dramatically reduce the amount of uncertainty involved.

In fact, one of the problems with prediction markets is their very newness because, as with any novel idea, you may encounter resistance. It's not uncommon for people to think prediction markets could never be as accurate as their own estimates, and that's due to the illusion of control. It's a bit like those who don't believe that travelling by plane is actually safer than driving your own car. Why? Because when we drive a car we believe that we're in control. The chances of being injured or killed are much higher when driving a car when compared with being a passenger in a plane, but people still hold the belief they are safer on the ground. In just the same way, it's common for people to trust their own intuition more than they ever trust the market, where they clearly can't control the outcome.

How to use prediction markets

So how does the use of prediction markets fit with everything else covered in Part II of this book? In a nutshell, prediction markets work as a source of information. Consider scenario analysis (Chapter 8), which looks at the probability around one seminal event. When scenario analysis asks, 'What is the value outcome if said event doesn't work out?', then goes on to ask, 'What if it does?', a prediction market can help you weigh this sort of discussion.

Similarly, you can use prediction markets in conjunction with stochastic analysis (Chapter 9), as this is basically an extension or a more sophisticated version of scenario analysis. This is especially true when it's not a clear-cut outcome you're measuring but a continuous one.

In fact, the only place in Part II where prediction markets won't work is with sensitivity analysis (Chapter 7) because sensitivity analysis only assumes an arbitrary change. Prediction markets are best used as a source of information that you can plug into a scenario or stochastic analysis; this is where their real value lies.

KEY TAKEAWAYS

→ Under certain circumstances, prediction markets are more accurate at predicting the future than any one individual opinion.

→ However, with any aggregate of opinion you should always beware the herd mentality.

→ Where external prediction markets don't exist you can always create internal markets or simply gauge sentiment using online tools such as Google, Twitter and Facebook.

→ Although prediction markets do not guarantee a particular result — they only give an indication of how probable it is — they are still an invaluable tool for business valuation.

FURTHER READING

James Surowiecki, *The Wisdom of Crowds: Why the Many Are Smarter Than the Few and How Collective Wisdom Shapes Business, Economies, Societies and Nations*, Random House, New York, 2004.

Douglas W. Hubbard, *Pulse: The New Science of Harnessing Internet Buzz to Track Threats and Opportunities*, Wiley & Sons, Hoboken, 2011.

Part III

How can I
increase value?

Chapter 11

Real value adding compared to 'pump and dump'

It is our choices that show what we truly are ...
— JK Rowling, *Harry Potter and the Chamber of Secrets*

Back in the 18th century the world was Britain's oyster. It was a time of extreme prosperity for the island nation, so when the South Sea Company — the first ever limited stock company — was founded in 1711, attracting investors was like shooting fish in a barrel. The South Sea Company enjoyed a monopoly trade with the Spanish colonies in South America, and soon after its inception the company underwrote the British national debt (at the time over £10 million) on the promise of 6 per cent interest from the government. Shares in the South Sea Company rose to 10 times their value and a wave of investor frenzy ensued (even Sir Isaac Newton jumped on board). This wave of speculation was exacerbated by the company directors talking up rumours of South Sea riches. Consequently, the share prices in the South Sea Company grew, over the course of a single year, from approximately £100 to almost £1000 per share.

> ❝ Essentially — for all the main drivers — your forecast error is likely to be large if you assume much greater than your current performance. ❞

You won't be surprised to hear then that, given its success, the South Sea Bubble was not the only bubble floating around in 1720. As overall interest in joint stock investment grew, the British market was flooded with new ventures, each creating their own small bubble. Some of these bubbles now appear downright ridiculous, such as the company that was reportedly floated to buy Irish bogs, or the company manufacturing a gun to fire square cannonballs, or another promising to 'carry out an undertaking of great advantage but nobody is to know what it is!' (Unbelievably, this lofty objective attracted £2000 in investment.)

However, the tide began to turn in the summer of 1720 because the directors of the South Sea Company realised that their shares didn't accurately reflect the value of the company. So they bailed. As other shareholders got wind of this, panicked selling ensued, and when the South Sea Bubble burst that year its collapse was swift and severe.

The South Sea Company is a classic case in the study of asset price bubbles. In fact, in their book *Manias, Panics and Crashes: A History of Financial Crises*, Kindleberger and Aliber rank the South Sea Bubble as number two in their list of 'the big 10 financial bubbles' in history (number one being The Dutch Tulip Bulb Bubble of 1636).[43] Accordingly, the South Sea is a fitting place to start the third section of this book.

> It's vital, then, to recognise that your results can return to the mean very quickly.

Part III and the poker table

In Part III we look at ways of adding real value to your company rather than just the 'pump and dump' manipulation of share prices. It's important to understand from the outset that when talking about adding value, I'm not talking about getting people overexcited about value like those poor suckers who invested in the South Sea Bubble. I'm talking about improving the cash flows of your business in excess of the risk that those cash flows are exposed to. In other words, adding value is about making real changes that improve the overall competitive advantage of your business.

In order to do this, we'll stop by the poker table frequently because poker is a powerful analogy for strategy, given that it is a highly strategic game (much more so than other forms of gambling such as blackjack). In fact, in the fantastic book *The Poker Face of Wall Street*, author Aaron Brown asserts: 'Gambling lies at the heart of economic ideas and institutions ... Not surprisingly, the game most like the financial markets — poker — is hugely popular with financial professionals. Poker has valuable lessons for winning in the markets, and markets have equally valuable lessons for winning at poker'.[44]

Here, I should lay my cards on the table and profess to sitting comfortably in that category. I enjoy playing poker, as do many of my colleagues in valuation; it's little wonder when you consider how much strategic thought is involved in the game.

To illustrate how Part III, and poker, fits with the rest of the book, let's recap what we've covered so far.

Part I: This section discussed the various valuation techniques that enable you to come up with a dollar figure for your business. We learnt how to ascertain what any business is worth.

Part II: Here we used the valuation figure from Part I to determine what you can expect to receive in the future (i.e. the expected valuation of the business), as well as how much variation you can expect around this average.

Now in Part III, we'll again take the valuation figure provided by Parts I and II and look at how you go about improving that number, because this is the ultimate objective of most people in business. You can consider the title of this chapter as a good indicator of where this entire section is headed. Because, if you finish reading Part III with an understanding of the actions you can take to improve the intrinsic value of your business, then I'll have done my job.

> Pump and dump is a scheme that attempts to boost the price of a stock temporarily through rumour and false recommendations.

Real value versus 'pump and dump'

Much has been written about the difficulties of determining market value, most notably about how market value doesn't necessarily add up to intrinsic value. So what's the difference between real value and 'pump and dump'?

Pump and dump is a scheme that attempts to boost the price of a stock temporarily through rumour and false recommendations. The offenders in a pump and dump scheme, who already have a stake in the company, generally sell their shares only after their manipulation has inflated the share price (just as with the South Sea Bubble). The practice of pump and dump is illegal, not to mention highly unethical. Plus, this very nasty trading activity tends to have an extremely short shelf life because the public has a way of finding out about these things very quickly.

In the online and highly connected world we occupy today, pump and dump schemes still occasionally come to light, usually as part of a broader scam. For example, online financial dictionary Investopedia provides an example of a pump and dump scheme carried out in the USA through cold calling.[45] The internet is now a much more common method of scamming investors. In this case, though, victims received a message on their answering machines that talked up a hot stock tip, but the message was left in such a way that it sounded like it had been left for the wrong person by accident.

Pump and dump schemes often target micro- and small-cap stocks, because these are usually the easiest to influence.[46] Stocks where there's a lot of uncertainty, such as mining, early-stage technologies or pharmaceutical companies, are also ripe for this sort of manipulation. There are plenty of other examples of pump and dump scams around but I'm not going to get into those here. Suffice to say, if this is the game you're in then this isn't the book for you.

The problem with price

What I do want to point out here is the difficulty we often have in establishing prices because we all revert to relative comparisons (see William Poundstone's book *The Myth of Fair Value* for more on this). Humans find it inherently difficult to weigh up comparative value. For instance, if you're in the market for a new car and you've just test-driven a Ferrari, a Porsche will look cheap by comparison. But consider for a moment that a Porsche probably costs around 30 times the price of a Hyundai Getz and that the Getz will do the same job (albeit not in as much style, by some people's measure). Is the Porsche really worth 30 times as much as the Getz?

> If you're in the market for a new car and you've just test-driven a Ferrari, a Porsche will look cheap by comparison.

When it comes to product pricing, the result is that there's a lot of room for movement. There's a great deal of scope for companies to capture or create value in the minds of shareholders because people generally find price comparisons very difficult. But, again, that's not the aim of this section. I'm not interested in taking advantage of people's biases or psychological flaws and conjuring value where it doesn't really exist. What this book is about is creating value that's really worth something.

Real value adding

Having determined the difference between real value versus cheap pump and dump, we reach the million-dollar question: How do you really create superior returns for shareholders, which then drives premium value? In other words, how do you add real value?

There are several elements involved in achieving real value. These include decisions around these questions:

→ Where do you participate? Or, what are your portfolio choices?
→ How do you compete?
→ How do you operate? What choices do you have in terms of processes?
→ How do you finance your business?
→ Finally, value is not just about expectations of the future but about how well you deliver against those expectations. So how do you execute, communicate and manage your value?

Graphically, these elements (and Part III) look like this.

Chapter 12 **Portfolio choices** Which business are you in?		
Chapter 13 **Competitive choices** Where do you plan to compete?	**Chapter 14** **Operating choices and execution** How do you plan to operate and deliver?	**Chapter 15** **Financing choices** Where do you plan to get the money?
Chapter 16 **Communicating value** How well do you communicate your plans and the actions they give rise to? How do you communicate outcomes?		

As you can imagine, different businesses enjoy advantages in different areas; again, this is not unlike poker. Just as there are various elements contributing to strategy, there are multiple components in poker, and the skill lies in playing these to your advantage.

> Sensitivity analysis is invaluable for identifying exactly which key factors you need to understand and focus on within your business.

As Chapter 12 shows in greater detail, some people are able to compete solely on their ability to make successful portfolio choices. Take Warren Buffett for example. At last count, the inimitable investor was worth $47 billion (making him the third wealthiest person on the globe), in no small part because of his savvy investment decisions. In poker terms, selecting portfolio is akin to choosing which games you play, as well as the hands you play within those games.

Other people are highly adept at designing the way they compete in an industry (see Chapter 13). Google is a prime example. In fact, Google didn't just make some smart competitive choices; they effectively reinvented a whole industry when, as a fledgling brand back in 1998, Google took the way people thought about information and turned it on its head. Now the company is enjoying revenue to the tune of $8.58 billion.[47] Think of the competitive decision as how you choose to play each individual hand in poker.

> This sort of analysis ensures it's very easy to defend your conclusions to others by making it simple to explain why your answer is at least reasonable.

Yet others' talents lie in simply running a business. In Chapter 14 we explore the four elements of operation and see, in particular, how PwC strives for efficiency in its core process of recruitment. Next, to see financial efficiency in action (Chapter 15), we take a look at financing businesses, such as private equity houses, which use leverage and structuring to great effect. At the poker table, where you're limited to playing within your bankroll, financial choice is similarly all about how you finance yourself.

Finally, communication is all-important when it comes to creating value: there really is a skill to communicating the way your business delivers value. Until recently, for example, Leightons has shown itself proficient at delivery and communication. Leightons, an Australian construction and engineering company, runs a business in a highly competitive industry. However, over many years it's become known in the investment markets for being very good at delivering exactly what it sets out to do. Recently, though, as a result of some well-publicised issues, this perception has changed, emphasising the fragility of reputation for delivery.

As Chapter 16 demonstrates, there are three key things to remember when it comes to communicating a business's value. The first is that share price is simply a view of the future and people will have an expectation of what this future should look like. A future that turns out rosier than expected (i.e. a positive surprise in terms of share price) will leave shareholders satisfied yet, on the flip side, not only will a negative surprise leave shareholders dissatisfied but this disappointment will be more heavily weighted than any positive news might have been. That is, we tend to be more affected by bad news than good news. Any previous gains in share prices will quickly be forgotten when a poor result arrives, and shareholders will be reticent to trust you again. Consequently, the way you deliver your company's performance has a value benefit to the share price. Wesfarmers, for example, particularly before its acquisition of Coles in 2007, had a very good track record of delivering what it promised and enjoyed a premium weighting in its valuation. That premium weighting was in no small part down to its reliability in execution and delivery. However, as Shakespeare's Othello so eloquently put it (and as I'm sure Wesfarmers is acutely aware), it's all too possible to lose your reputation, or 'the immortal part' of one's self, much faster than you can gain it.

The second point in communicating a business's value is that valuation must be understood in order to be relevant. If you've got a great business but no-one knows about it, it's hardly likely to be valuable because value is a communal, not an individual, concept. Therefore, the way in which you talk about your business, and the type and extent of information you provide to your investors, is a very effective means of realising value. I'm not saying you should create value in this way, because all you're doing is reporting the facts, but you can certainly help to realise it by communicating well.

Finally, and most importantly, bad news well told is a form of good communication too. There seems to be some confusion about the concept of effective communication: many people believe it's only ever delivering good news. Not true. We all know life doesn't run according to plan. Results will be poor, markets will fall seemingly inexplicably and there will always be times when we cannot deliver what we'd hoped to. If you communicate effectively upfront by telling shareholders what your strategy is, what the risks are and how you plan to manage any potential problems, you might just save yourself some headaches with disgruntled shareholders further down the track. According to the stereotype, politicians offer a quintessential example of how not to do this. How many times have you heard a politician deny there was a problem in the first place? Or break a promise? Or backflip on a policy issue? Too many times to count, I'm sure.

Warren Buffett, on the other hand, again provides us with something to aspire to. In 2011 Buffett lost one of his most trusted senior executives and a potential successor, David Sokol, over allegations of insider trading. Having previously said of Sokol: 'I can't overstate the breadth and importance of Dave Sokol's achievements at this company,'[48] Buffett was forced to make a very public about-turn after his advisor's shock resignation. Yet a situation that could have quickly spiralled into scapegoating by Buffett distancing himself from Sokol was very effectively avoided by Buffett's characteristic straight-shooting communication. On why he didn't push Sokol for answers over his acquisition of a chemical maker, Buffett said, 'I obviously made a big mistake not saying, "Well, when did you buy it?"'[49] A great example of why good communication isn't just about telling good news.

KEY TAKEAWAYS

→ Pump and dump schemes attempt to boost the price of stock by hyping false, misleading or greatly exaggerated claims.

→ By contrast, value adding is about making real changes that improve the overall competitive advantage of your business.

→ There are several elements involved in achieving real value. These include decisions around participation or portfolio choices; competitive choices; operating choices; financing choices; and executing, communicating and managing your value.

→ The way you deliver and communicate your company's performance has a value benefit to the share price.

FURTHER READING

William Poundstone, *Priceless: The Myth of Fair Value (and How to Take Advantage of It)*, Hill & Wang, New York, 2010.

Charles P. Kindleberger and Robert Z. Aliber, *Manias, Panics and Crashes: A History of Financial Crises (5th edition)*, Wiley & Sons, Hoboken, 2005.

Aaron Brown, *The Poker Face of Wall Street*, Wiley & Sons, Hoboken, 2006.

Chapter 12

Portfolio choices

*The race is not always to the swift nor
the battle to the strong, but that's the way to bet.*
— Damon Runyon, American newspaperman and writer

There are two golden rules when it comes to playing poker. The first, and at the risk of sounding facetious, is to pick an easy game. In Texas hold 'em (a variation of poker), selecting the table to play is often the major determinant of whether you'll be a winning player or not. If you choose a game where you know all the other players are less skilled, you're more likely to win that game. Whereas by playing against gun players you're not in an advantaged game and chances are you'll lose just as many times as you win (assuming you're even as adept as your opponents). While this type of game might be more fun to play, it's hardly likely to be remunerative, so the first rule of poker is to pick a game where you're the best player. It also helps if the other (less able players) are wealthy. This is the Promised Land as far as Texas hold 'em is concerned.

> Scenario analysis should be integrated into our valuation analysis so that, rather than focus on how right we are, we look at how wrong we can be.

Secondly, you should play tight aggressive. This is the most frequently quoted winning strategy in hold 'em and involves choosing only a few hands to bet on and betting only where you have a major advantage. It follows that when you do bet, you should invest a substantial amount.

Conversely, there will be many times in poker when you choose not to bet because it's clear you don't have an advantage. Here, as the adage goes, it's best to quit when you're still well and truly ahead. In Texas hold 'em, for example, the best time to fold is just after the private cards have been dealt rather than holding out as the stakes rise. Pundits suggest that the most effective way to improve your winning percentages is to be really judicious about which hands you bet on after you have received your private cards. In playing a tight-aggressive strategy, you should always get dealt your cards but be disciplined in focusing on where your advantage lies because it's better to cut your losses before you get in too deep.

As you may have already recognised, portfolio choices are much like poker. In fact, so striking are the similarities in terms of skills required that hedge-fund recruiters have been known to scout games of Texas hold 'em looking for potential employees.

Case study: from the poker table to the board table

So how do we take what we've learned from poker and apply it to the corporate environ? You can't go past Jack Welch, former CEO of the General Electric (GE) Company, for an outstanding example. Jack began his career with GE in 1960 and by 1981 was the company's chairman and CEO. The golden child of corporate America for years, Welch took on GE when it was in difficult times and turned it into one of the most successful US companies in the past half a century.

His strategy? Welch did exactly what any poker player would do.

First, he disposed of all of GE's bad hands so that anything that wasn't producing value (and was unlikely to do so in the future) was sold. In fact, so ruthless was Welch in this phase that he earned the moniker 'Neutron Jack' for the rate at which he eliminated employees. In his book *Jack: Straight from the Gut*, Welch states that GE went from 411,000 employees in 1980 to 229,000 by 1985[50] and that he was rumoured to have fired the bottom 10 per cent of his managers each year.[51] Essentially, he was sorting out which hands he was going to play.

> Scenario analysis allows you to examine a whole suite of circumstances that could change.

Next, Welch determined that GE was going to be number one and number two in every market it participated in, otherwise it would get out of that market completely. That takes us back to playing a tight-aggressive game, or betting on hands where you know you have an advantage.

The result? Welch was one of the most successful business strategists ever in terms of practical outcomes. During his tenure as CEO at GE, the company's market capitalisation increased from $13 billion to $400 billion[52] and in 2000 he was named 'Manager of the Century' by *Fortune* magazine.

Making portfolio choices

Having seen the success Jack Welch found with poker strategies, the key question for us all is: How can I do that?

While I can't promise you market capitalisation of $400 billion, the following three sections offer valuable methods for making portfolio choices and will help you to build a useful picture of your business.

Industry attractiveness

In order to make effective portfolio choices, you should first look at which markets your business competes in and then select your games accordingly. This is best done by constructing a grid that analyses growth compared to average, or GDP (because the economy's growth is a helpful proxy for the average), and economic profitability.

Figure 33: Industry attractiveness

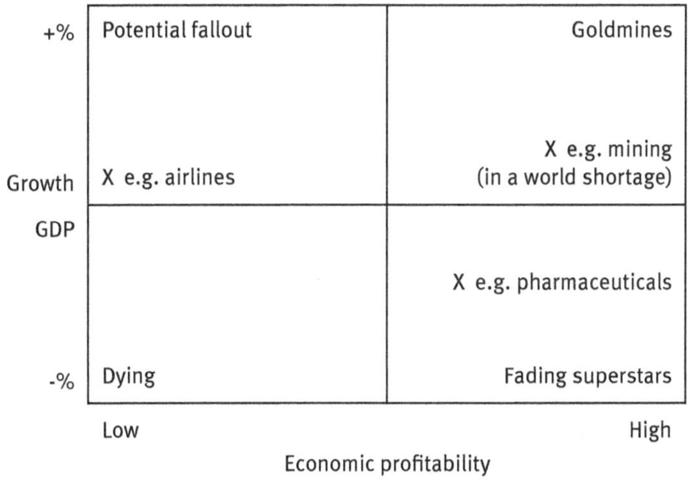

Some industries are growing, but it is difficult for individual companies within them to make money. For example, the airline industry, which would be located in the potential fallout quadrant and is marked on the figure above with an 'X'. Due to a fall in prices, as well as the increased frequency with which people are flying now, there is still considerable growth in the airline game; it is just that no-one is making much money. Yet growth without profitability can't last forever, hence the potential for fallout (though hopefully not from the sky).

Other industries, such as the pharmaceuticals industry, could be classified as being in decline, or 'fading superstars', as they reach the end of long patent cycles. Again, there's not much growth, but occasionally there is some profitability here. Yet others are growing fast but their business structure is weak, so they should be wary of potential fallout (although for consumers, they could just as easily be called 'consumer delights'). Finally, certain industries do exist where it seems profit and growth go hand in hand; industries such as mining, which is growing at an enormous rate and enjoying bumper profits, making them 'gold mines' in more ways than one.

Choosing which industry to participate in is much like selecting which game of poker to play. You need to ensure that you're choosing the right game (or games), so examine the economics of the industry carefully before committing to play at that table. This involves taking into consideration growth and profitability and asking two key questions:

i)   Is the demand for this industry growing?

ii)   Can people profit in this industry?

In other words, make sure you place your bets in good games.

Portfolio actions

Having determined which games to play, you next need to understand how your business compares so that — within those games — you're betting where you have an advantage.

> During financial crises, instead of no correlation, things suddenly start to become highly correlated.

The matrix below will assist you in deciding where to play.

Figure 34: Portfolio actions

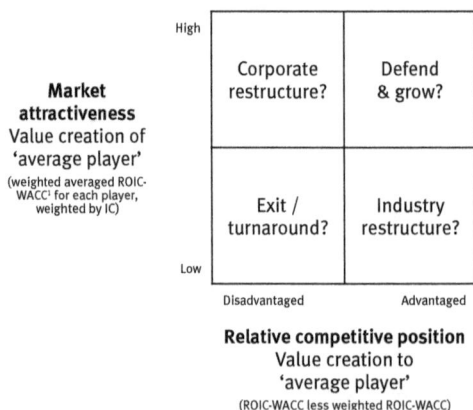

In the 'Industry Restructure' quadrant, while your relative competitive position may be favourable, the market you're trading in is not. If you're operating in this space it's imperative to ask exactly how much of an economic profit you are making. Is it possible that you're thriving in an industry that's fundamentally unattractive? Here, there are a couple of different strategies available to you.

First, you could buy out your competitors with the aim of transforming them while effectively rearranging the capacity of the market to make it even more profitable for you. Or you could just wait for the other competitors to collapse (an eventuality that's not unreasonable). Coles Group Limited and Wesfarmers Limited recently went through this exact process with their own comprehensive restructure within the retail sector. Upon examining the sector, Wesfarmers decided that, despite being one of only a few major players in an attractive industry, Coles was not making money as it should have been. In response to that analysis, Wesfarmers acquired Coles in 2007 with a view to restructuring the industry. After a comprehensive turnaround process and some GFC-related difficulties, the integration of the Coles Group is now widely considered to have been a success.

But what if you're already in a sector that's successful? In the second quadrant, 'Defend and Grow', participants enjoy an industry that's profitable and a business that's performing better than average. However, anyone sitting here needs an effective strategy to protect their current position. Ask yourself: Are there barriers to prevent new competitors from entering this space?

A favoured strategy to defend and grow your business is to head off any potential threats. For example, Facebook purchased Instagram, and Microsoft scooped up Skype. Both actions can be read as a defensive mechanism designed to protect their own franchises through acquisition.

The situation is vastly different, however, if you find yourself in a business that's performing badly and an industry that's worse. Anyone unlucky enough to fall into the 'Exit/Turnaround' quadrant should think like a poker player and know when to quit. While I don't want to name names here, I'm sure you can call to mind many high-profile examples of businesses that fit this bill.

Instead, let's look at the 'Corporate Restructure' quadrant. Here things are slightly rosier but the strategy is the same because, even though you might be in an industry that's profitable, if your business itself is failing you should probably still get out. Consider: Do I have a realistic chance of being able to salvage the business? Is there anything I can realistically do? Or am I wiser to sell to someone else who can use my assets better than I can? Here, and as we learned at the poker table, it's important to be selective about which hands you play.

Capital deployment

The third and final component of portfolio choices is capital deployment. Earlier we talked about how to manage your bankroll and be savvy about where you place your bets in poker. In corporate strategy, it's similarly important to understand exactly where your bets are laid in your market. For this, we use the following analysis.

Figure 35: Capital deployment

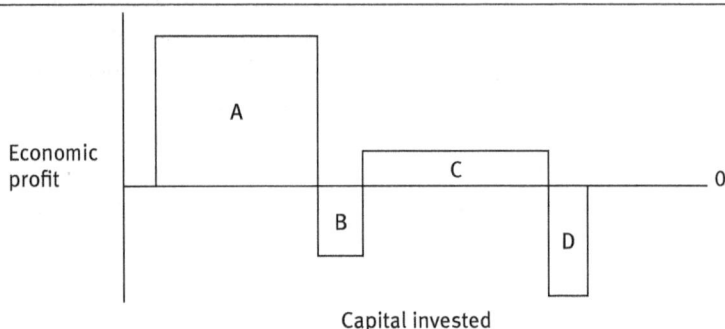

Capital invested

This graph allows you to view the amount of capital you have invested (i.e. where your bets are), as well as how much economic profit you're enjoying in each of those businesses. While it's important to business growth for you to experiment with new ideas, or play several small hands, you should never tie up too much capital in a hand you're not confident of winning. Ideally, you'll invest as much money as possible in those areas where you're advantaged.

Using the capital deployment matrix, you are able to see where all your capital is invested, which, in turn, reveals anywhere you're not making an economic profit; here, you should channel 'Neutron Jack' and cut your losses. In other words, always make sure you're playing a tight-aggressive game.

As my colleague John Studley says, this applies not only at a business level but also at project, product and customer level too.

Take, for example, the scenario above. This particular company has four investments (A, B, C and D) and — considering the sum total of those investments — its overall performance is fairly average. Most of this organisation's investment is tied up in two ventures that are returning at above the cost of capital (A and C). Yet these are being dragged down by the remaining investments (B and D), which aren't performing well at all. The best way for this company to improve overall performance, and to improve it significantly, is to restructure those two ventures that aren't up to scratch.

So you can see that in moving from the poker table to the board table, you can take along a great many lessons. Most importantly, and in order to increase value, always bet where economic conditions are favourable and minimise your bets where they're not.

To determine where this is, it's advisable to carry out the three analyses covered in this chapter, which build on the economic analyses covered in Part I:

i)   industry attractiveness — understand the industry you're in (from the point of view of growth and profitability on average)

ii) portfolio actions — understand how your business compares

iii) capital deployment — understand where your bets are laid.

Moreover, to really maximise value, always play by the golden rules of poker:

→ Wherever possible, place your bets in good games. Within those games, make sure you bet only where you have an advantage.

→ When you've got a disadvantage within your industry, or you're in a bad game, always be ready to cut your losses.

KEY TAKEAWAYS

→ There are two golden rules when it comes to playing poker that just as easily apply to portfolio choices: pick an easy game and play tight aggressive.

→ The first step to making effective portfolio choices is to examine which markets your business competes in and then select your games accordingly.

→ In determining your portfolio actions, it's important to understand how your business compares in terms of market attractiveness and competitive position so that you're always betting where you have an advantage.

→ Using the capital deployment analysis, you should examine where your capital lies and where you're not turning an economic profit so you can always make sure you're playing a tight-aggressive game.

→ In order to increase value always bet where economic conditions are favourable and minimise your bets where they're not.

FURTHER READING

Aaron Brown, *The Poker Face of Wall Street*, Wiley & Sons, Hoboken, 2006.

William Poundstone, *Fortune's Formula: The Untold Story of the Scientific Betting System that Beat the Casinos and Wall Street*, Hill & Wang, New York, 2005.

Chapter 13

Competitive choices

And while the law of competition may be sometimes hard for the individual, it is best for the race, because it ensures the survival of the fittest in every department.
— Andrew Carnegie, Scottish-American industrialist

Dubbed 'the greatest gun fighter in the American Old West', James Butler 'Wild Bill' Hickok was a lawman of mixed repute. However, 'Wild Bill' was not just a gunslinger but also a gun player, possessing a penchant for professional poker. On 2 August 1876, Hickok was playing poker at Nuttal & Mann's Saloon No. 10 in Deadwood, Black Hills, Dakota Territory when he found himself clutching a 'dead man's hand'. A poker hand that is, comprising a pair of aces and a pair of eights, all black.

> Examine which markets your business competes in and then select your games accordingly.

Despite its name, 'a dead man's hand' is a good hand to hold (or it was at the time 'Wild Bill' was playing poker), so 'Wild Bill' was most likely all set to win the game in Deadwood when he encountered what is called in poker 'a bad beat'. This is when you've got a great set of cards but still lose, through sheer bad luck. As 'Wild Bill' sat with his back to the saloon doors on that fateful day, 'Broken Nose Jack' McCall barged in, drew his pistol and shot 'Wild Bill' in the back of the head, killing him instantly.

Now, there's no way 'Wild Bill' could have known that his 'dead man's hand' would soon be lying in his own dead hand and that he would be beaten in the worst possible way. But his tale does serve to remind us that it doesn't matter how good your hand might be, you should always be aware of what's happening around you. In particular, what games other people might be playing.

You see, there are two prerequisites to winning at poker: having a good hand, and knowing if your competitor's hand is better. Sounds simple, doesn't it? Yet so many players — in poker and in business — focus exclusively on the first half of this equation. When playing poker, it's important to be dealt a good hand, to understand what a good hand is and to know what to do to improve your hand (for instance, having a working understanding of how the suits work together). But it's just as vital, through the process of betting, to gather information about your competitor's hand so you're able to react accordingly. While it's important to know that a royal flush is the best hand you could possibly want, you must also try to learn what your competitors' hands are and whether they can trump you.

This is a good analogy for competitive choices in business. In this chapter, we learn about the elements of a good hand or the suits of competitive strength, how to recognise them when you've got them and how to improve them when you don't.

We also examine competitive choices as a relative not an absolute game, because this is one of the biggest downfalls of competitive analysis to date: the failure to consider the reaction of your competitors. Just like poker, competitive strategy is comparative: it's not enough to score a really good hand and then to play that hand well. Effective competitive choices take into account the other players as well, and that's where the game really starts to get interesting.

Elements of competitive strategy

First, however, let's start with the elements of competitive strategy. The suits of competitive advantage — or COPS, if you will — are:
→ Costs and business/operating model
→ Offer (i.e. what do you offer to the customer?)
→ Price (i.e. what is the price point of your offer?)
→ Segments (i.e. which section of the market are you competing in?)

> It's important to understand how your business compares in terms of market attractiveness and competitive position so that you're always betting where you have an advantage.

What's interesting is not how each of these elements works in isolation but how they interact. For example, employing a low-cost model but charging a high price for your offering would not really work for your customers, so it is not sustainable. Throw in the added complication of a customer segment that values quality and suddenly your plan is looking decidedly incongruous.

Just like in poker, it doesn't matter how good any one card is; the cards in your hand need to work in combination with one another if they're to be of any use to you. Your king, queen, jack and ace, for instance, are all great cards but if there is no 10, they're not much good to you. Moreover, if someone else has four threes in their hand (one from every suit), for all the low denomination of their cards they will trump yours, simply because their cards work in concert with one another.

> As in poker, it doesn't matter how good any one card is; the cards in your hand need to work in combination with one another if they're to be of any use to you.

Traditionally, many competitive strategies only examine these COPS elements singly and in turn, rather than in combination, which is a significant shortcoming in my eyes. Not only that, for the longest time many organisations have seemed preoccupied with cost at the expense of the other elements, such as the offer they put to the market, the price they charge or the segments they compete in. While this appears to be changing now, as people recognise the importance of all of the various elements of competition, there is still a way to go and any improvements you can make here will offer you very real ways to add value.

Three models of competitive strategy

Before we look at each of the four COPS elements in detail, and given we've just learned how important correlation between the elements is, let's cover the three models of competitive strategy and see how COPS can work together. Remember Michael Porter from Chapter 2 ('Conducting a strategic and financial analysis')? According to Porter there are really only three possible configurations of the COPS elements for you to choose from:

I) Low-cost model — here, companies compete for business on the basis of price. By providing the cheapest possible offering, organisations using this model aim to beat all competitors by matching price with lowest cost.

ii) Differentiate — businesses using the differentiation model put together an offer and a price package that is so unique it's more desirable and justifies a price in excess of its costs.

iii) Niche — this model ascribes to the idea that businesses should sell an offering that's tailored to one particular segment of the market, with costs and revenues designed to make money in just that segment.[53]

Graphically, Porter's three models look like this.

Figure 36: Models of competitive strategy

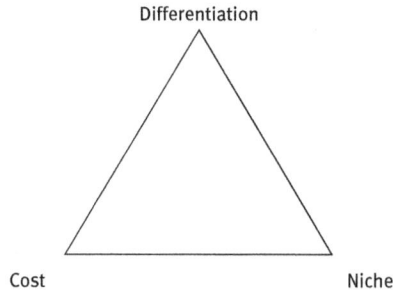

Differentiation

Cost   Niche

In a low-cost situation, your expenses are minimised, so your offer will be relatively basic compared with the rest of the market and, subsequently, the segments you appeal to will be fairly broad. If you're a motorcycle rider like I am, a Hyosung would fit the bill here, because it's a cheap and cheerful bike that's targeted towards entry-level riders.

By contrast, a differentiation model might involve a higher-cost product, such as a Ducati motorcycle, which is intended for a more discerning market.

A niche product would be something like a Harley Davidson, which is very heavily branded and directed at a specialised target market. Fans of the movie *Easy Rider*, for starters.

In order to implement your competitive strategy successfully, you need to ensure you're competing in a market size and segment that matches your cost and pricing requirements. There's no point trying to appeal to a broad segment if you're offering a niche product because, by very definition, the two are contradictory. Of course, with the advent of e-commerce (and the flexibility this offers) online retailers can now enjoy niche markets as small as one single person. For more details on the rise of niche markets see *The Long Tail: Why the Future of Business is Selling Less of More* by Chris Anderson.

Costs

Now let's run through each of the various elements of competitive strategy in detail, starting with costs. The costs of your business model are generally determined by the composition of your value chain. For instance, how do you source your raw materials? Do you manufacture and if so, how is this performed? How do you deliver your product? How do you service your customers? What's your mode of selling? Usually, the more complex your business model the more costly your production. For example, if you offer a really personalised product, such as a bespoke suit, this will be more expensive to produce than a suit that's bought straight off the rack due to the time and production involved.

Added to this is the technology used in your production process. Anything sewn by hand will clearly be much more expensive than clothing that's produced by machine; however, you might be prepared to fork out for this if you can identify a niche market that demands bespoke fashion.

Then, of course, there are natural advantages that exist. Say you're able to corner the global market for cashmere production: then suddenly you might just be able to produce cashmere suits much more efficiently and cheaply than your competitors and so the cost advantage is all yours.

Finally, experience and scale both have a significant impact on cost. If you're lucky enough to provide services that incur only marginal costs to the business, you can enjoy economies of scale or scale advantages over your competitors. For instance, in telecommunications, in certain segments it's much cheaper for incumbent providers to deliver some services to their customers than it is for their smaller competitors. On top of this, experience can prove invaluable. Going back to our suit analogy, I'm sure if I had to make a suit it would take me months just to learn the process involved, let alone put needle to thread, whereas a tailor who had been creating hand-crafted suits all his life could probably whip up a dinner suit in a day if pressed (excuse the pun).

Given the variables involved in cost, there are plenty of options available to you to develop a cost strategy that's perfectly suited to your business, but do remember that your costs must be in alignment with all the other elements of your competitive strategy. One of the best-known examples of a misaligned strategy came from the Italian fashion powerhouse Gucci. In the 1980s Gucci markedly reduced the price of its offerings in a bid to conquer more of the market. What Gucci failed to realise, however, was that its customers were mostly attracted to the brand for its perceived exclusivity.[54] By slashing its prices and trying to attract a broader market segment, Gucci only succeeded in alienating its traditional market — while failing to attract new customers because its prices were still comparatively high. As with all the elements of competitive strategy, the trick with cost is always to focus on how it fits within your bigger competitive picture.

Offer

The second of our COPS elements of competition is offer, and there are three factors to be considered:

    i)   **Function** — this relates to the function or purpose of what it is you're offering. For instance, at its most basic, the function of a suit is to keep your customers warm, dry and clothed.

    ii)   **Fit** — what other impacts does your product offer? That same suit that's keeping your customer warm and dry might allow them, indirectly, to earn a greater salary by awarding them a more professional appearance in the workplace. So ask yourself: What is the economic impact of the product you're selling?

    iii) **Fashion** — finally, what does the product say about the individual customer? Say you're selling a high-end suit, as opposed to a suit you might wear to a raucous Bachelor & Spinster's ball. Despite having essentially the same function, those two products say vastly different things about who your customers are and, as such, will appeal to vastly different people.

Price

Next is the issue of price. Huge amounts of value can be unleashed by your choice of pricing strategy because there are three levels of pricing and three issues within those levels that need to be considered, presenting numerous possible combinations.

The three levels of pricing are outlined here.

Industry-wide pricing

At the broadest level, you should examine how the costs of all competitors in your industry behave, as well as where your business sits relative to others' costs, and then price accordingly.

Market-based pricing

Again, this is all about relative value. For instance, if I go to the retail clothing market with a package of offers and it becomes apparent to me that people value exclusivity in a suit, it follows that I should price that exclusivity high in order to maintain it. A suit that's very exclusive should necessarily demand a high price in order to satisfy the market, whereas a suit that's not as exclusive will be awarded a lower price.

Ways to improve your market pricing position are shown below.

Figure 37: Analysis of market pricing

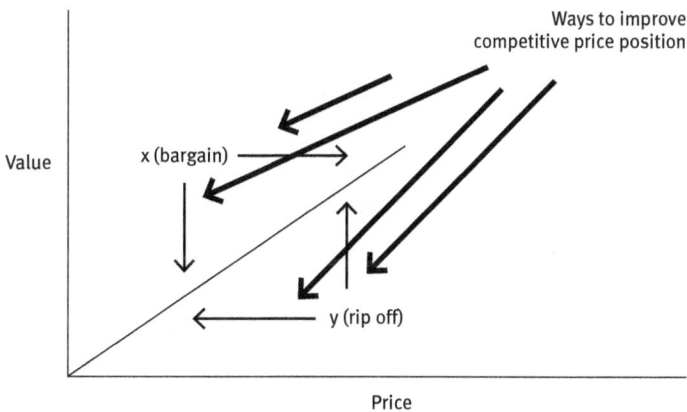

As you can see, the value function occupies the vertical axis, while price is on the horizontal. Ideally your product offerings will sit somewhere on this price/value curve. (Note that the price–value relationship is not necessarily a straight line.) So if you're offering your customers a bargain (that is, too much value for the price demanded), you should increase the price and follow the direction of the arrow to move closer to the demand curve, or reduce the value of your offer. For example, a common strategy (and one that I'm sure we've all seen in the supermarket) is when package sizes shrink but price doesn't change accordingly. In this way, businesses reduce the value of their offering while keeping the price the same.

Conversely, if your product is perceived by the market to be a 'rip-off' (not enough value for money spent) then you're necessarily going to lose market share if you don't change your price. Here, you either increase your value or decrease your price.

When considering price and value, you should spend some time thinking about what it is that drives value for your consumers, because it's not always the same for every product and across every market. This way you can adjust your pricing strategy accordingly. There are a range of analytical tools available to you, one of which is a conjoint analysis. A conjoint analysis is used to determine what it is that customers desire most. For instance, if you were designing a new car it would be pertinent to ask potential customers a series of questions like: If you had two cars and one had leather seats and the other didn't, would you pay extra for leather seating? If so, how much? This type of questioning should be carried out for a range of variables to enable you to build up a picture of the value function in your graph, which in turn allows you to map all relative competitive products and to ascertain just where it is in the marketplace that you sit.

Transactional pricing

Finally, there are a several tactical opportunities available to you in terms of the short-term pricing of products. A common example is discounting patterns that occur in large firms, such as off-peak discounting or end-of-season sales. Airlines are especially adept at this sort of yield management school of pricing and it's not uncommon to see major carriers discounting prices when their planes are not full. Similarly, power stations recognise the need to keep power constantly running so they'll accept a lower rate at off-peak times just to ensure consistent revenue.

Segment

The fourth of our COPS elements — segment — offers yet another way to modify your competitive strategy. The segment you operate in can be organised according to three variables:

i) The size of the segment.

ii)   The spend of the segment.
iii) The sensitivity of that segment to value. A simple way to improve your competitive position is to target your offer to the largest segment who values it most.

Competitive reactions

Having looked at each of the four elements of competition — costs, offer, price and segments — we can see that each variable of your offer must be aligned with the others. However, as mentioned at the outset, this is only one half of the equation when it comes to making competitive choices. The other half is the reactions of your competitors.

Why? Because business is a relative game, not an absolute one.

Previous iterations of competitive strategy fell down by ignoring the reactions of competitors. No strategic decision you ever make in business will fail to affect your competition, so do you really expect them not to respond? A great example is when a business cuts its prices on the assumption it'll gain more market share. Of course, such a plan completely misses the fact that its competitors will surely react by doing the same.

Effective competitive choices should always take into account the other players in your industry and must never work on the assumption that your competitors' positions are fixed. Going back to our poker analogy, if I've got a royal flush and I bet everything on that one hand only to find out someone else has a royal flush of a higher suit, suddenly my royal flush is irrelevant. In business as in poker, it pays to always be aware of what our competitors are doing.

Game theory

Back in Chapter 2 we looked at the movie *A Beautiful Mind*, which made famous the principles of John Forbes Nash Jr's game theory. The field of game theory is highly relevant for competitive choices as it recognises that competitive positioning is dynamic and extols the need to understand your competitors' strategies; understand the payoffs of your competitors' strategies; and know how a change in your strategy will affect your competitors — that is, how will it cause your competitors to react?

Increasingly, companies across many industries are using game theory as a way of understanding how their competitive position might change because of the reactions of others. Perhaps the best-known example is the prisoner's dilemma.

Prisoner's dilemma

This simple model has been used to teach game theory since its inception during the Cold War, but it's no less an effective analogy for competitive strategy today.

Figure 38: The prisoner's dilemma matrix

Player 1	Talk	0, 10	5, 5
	Shut up	0, 0	10, 0
		Shut up	Talk
		Player 2	

Say you and I have been arrested for a crime we committed. We're being held separately but the police have offered us the same deal, as shown by the prisoner's dilemma matrix. If I blow the whistle on you then you'll receive 10 years' imprisonment and I'll be allowed to walk free but if you blow the whistle on me, I'll receive 10 years' imprisonment and you'll walk free. If we both confess, we'll both receive five years' jail and if we both stay quiet then we'll both go free. Simple, really. If we both shut up it's a much better outcome for both of us; however, what's to say I'll keep quiet while you talk? If I think it's worth the gamble, I could walk free while you serve 10 years. The trick here is to know your competition well so you can predict (with some confidence) how they will react to any given situation, which is much like competitive strategy. When companies enter into a price or discounting war, their predicament is exactly the same as the prisoner's dilemma. If one discounts and the other doesn't follow suit, the former will eventually monopolise the market. (This is essentially the same as one prisoner talking while the other shuts up.) If both businesses discount, then both suffer diminished returns and the consumer is the only winner. Alternatively, if both businesses refrain from discounting then both are better off, proving that a price war rarely improves your competitive position.

Worth noting, however, is that game theory as depicted here represents a one-shot game. In reality, and where there are repeated games, businesses (like prisoners) are more likely to collaborate. Of course, in Australia the Australian Competition and Consumer Commission (ACCC) has very specific rules around competitive behaviour, and explicit collusion is hardly welcomed; even tacit collusion can be highly risky, and other jurisdictions have similar regulations.

You should always think carefully about the likely retaliation of your competitors to any strategy initiative. If you suddenly reduce your costs and then slash prices accordingly, how will that affect other players in the market? Is it likely they will take this lying down? It's not sufficient to consider your competitive options in isolation of what your rivals might do. Any attempt to improve your relative position should take into account the response of your competitors.

KEY TAKEAWAYS

→ The elements of competitive strategy — costs, offer, price and segment — need to be aligned in order to offer any real competitive advantage.

→ Competitive choices are relative, not absolute. Effective competitive choices should always take into account the other players in your industry and must never work on the assumption that your competitor's positions are fixed.

→ The field of game theory is highly relevant for competitive choices because it recognises that competitive positioning is dynamic.

→ Any competitive strategy should take into account the possible retaliation of competitors.

FURTHER READING

Chris Anderson, *The Long Tail: Why the Future of Business is Selling Less of More*, Hyperion, New York, 2006.

William Poundstone, *Priceless: The Myth of Fair Value (and how to take advantage of it)*, Hill & Wang, New York, 2010.

Thomas Nagle and Reed Holden, *The Strategy and Tactics of Pricing: A Guide to Profitable Decision Making (3rd edition)*, Prentice Hall, New York, 2001.

Michael Porter, *Competitive Strategy*, Free Press, New York, 1998.

Professor Robert Gibbons, *A Primer in Game Theory*, Financial Times/Prentice Hall, London, 1992.

David Besanks, David Dranove, Mark Shanley and Scott Schaeter, *Economics of Strategy (5th edition)*, Wiley & Sons, Hoboken, 2010.

Chapter 14

Operating choices and execution

Action is eloquence.
—William Shakespeare, *Coriolanus*

As Shakespeare so eloquently put it, actions speak louder than words. But it was Mark Twain who added that 'action speaks louder than words but not nearly as often'. Getting things done, it seems, is not easy.

Having examined which games you should play, plus how you play them in respect to other competitors, this chapter is dedicated to making sure your own technique (in business, just as in poker), is up to scratch. It offers a framework for making operating choices, as well as reflecting on how you organise yourself. It covers the four elements of operation, plus subsets of each. In essence, this chapter is all about getting stuff done.

Effective execution of strategy is vitally important because it's so common to have a great strategy but to fall down in its implementation. While it's naïve to underestimate the importance of strategy relative to execution (because both have a role to play), this chapter focuses exclusively on implementation and execution.

While so many value experts will tell you that if you simply shift your strategy from point A to point B you can add a lot of value, sometimes just getting things done is the hardest part. Those experts make the operation or execution part of the process read just like an economic assumption, assuming away the difficulties involved with implementation. Up there with the assumptions of consumer rationality and the economic equilibrium of price and quantity is the assumption that operating choices are easy to realise. True, we can often see where our business is now, as well as where we want it to be, but implementing the changes necessary to move from one to the other is never going to be easy. This chapter recognises that and, what's more, provides a framework to combat the gap between wishing things to be and actually having them done.

The third dimension: reality

Before we look at the framework I propose for operating choices, let's pause to examine one of the shortcomings of the traditional value-based management school of thought: there is no 'people dimension'.

The econocrats of this world would have us believe that a rational model of a firm's competitive advantages and strategic choices is all you need. While I agree that the value-based management model is a useful template that should be consulted because it has much to offer us, I'd argue that it's not the whole thesis and it doesn't capture reality in its messy entirety. As Polish–American scientist and philosopher Alfred Korzybski said, 'The map is not the territory'. The abstraction of the traditional value-based management model is just that: a model and not reality.

> These are not cards you're dealing with; these are real people with their own, very real will. The game of business is a much messier game than poker, and to ignore this fact by only using a rational strategic model is to do so at your peril.

In fact, there's a whole emerging school of thought that believes the value mindset is too rational, and the four elements of execution that we cover in this chapter offer a way to deal with the inevitable clash that occurs when these nice, clean models intersect with a messy reality.

The four elements of execution — leadership, core processes, initiatives and culture — are the tools that are available for you to influence and affect the resources at your disposal. Human resources, that is. To continue the poker analogy, these are not cards you're dealing with; these are real people with their own, very real will. The game of business is a much messier game than poker, and to ignore this fact by only using a rational strategic model is to do so at your peril.

All or nothing

Years ago two McKinsey partners, Peters and Waterman, wrote a very influential book — probably the bestselling business book ever — called *In Search of Excellence*. In it, the authors identified all the operations and behaviours common to effective organisations, and we discuss them in this chapter.

However, one of the criticisms of *In Search of Excellence* is that most of the companies given a gold star in the book have since lost their lustre. Without naming names or speculating on why these companies might have failed, there are two important lessons we can learn about implementing strategy.

1. There is no one right answer

Being of a business-value orientation, I'd argue that you can't simply identify any one of the four elements of execution as your means for increasing value. Instead, you need to do all of these things — leadership, core processes, initiatives and culture — well. Flexibility and agility are highly prized in valuation and you'll need to jockey between all of these four elements as the agenda of your situation dictates. This is one of the skills of the person who can manage value effectively. It's no good doing simply 'getting things done' but doing the wrong things, or implementing the right strategies but in the wrong areas; you need to get all four key areas of operation right in order to create value. However ...

2. It's all about priorities

At different stages throughout the business cycle and throughout the life cycle of your organisation, different facets of execution will take varying degrees of priority. The key here lies in choosing which issue is a priority at any one time, and this is what value is all about. There is a trade-off that's inherent in the very nature of value and, as this chapter shows, there are plenty of operational balls to be kept in the air. Because you can't achieve everything you want to at once, adding value becomes about being selective in your approach. This is the beauty of the value-based mindset: it gives you a framework in which you can effectively make those choices. It allows you to ask: What is the biggest issue affecting our business at the moment? Is it that our processes are so much more costly than our competitors'? Or is it that we own too many investments in poor competitive positions? It's important to recognise that effective execution is made up of a plethora of components (as the following framework shows) and that so many elements, naturally, require prioritisation.

A framework of execution

The framework shown here is the model I propose for taking your business bucket list and turning it into reality.

Figure 39: A framework for operating choices

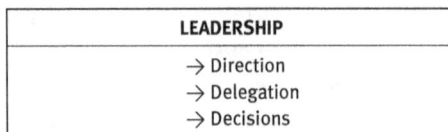

LEADERSHIP
→ Direction
→ Delegation
→ Decisions

Figure 39: A framework for operating choices (continued)

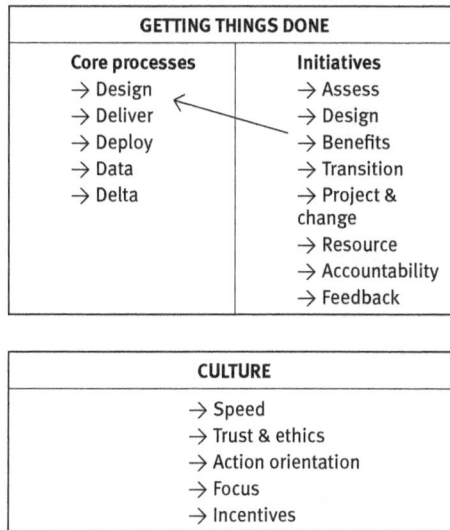

GETTING THINGS DONE	
Core processes	**Initiatives**
→ Design	→ Assess
→ Deliver	→ Design
→ Deploy	→ Benefits
→ Data	→ Transition
→ Delta	→ Project & change
	→ Resource
	→ Accountability
	→ Feedback

CULTURE
→ Speed
→ Trust & ethics
→ Action orientation
→ Focus
→ Incentives

As I said at the outset, I appreciate that executing strategy is much easier said than done, so let's look at each of the elements of this framework in turn, in an effort to make the challenge more palatable.

1. Leadership

From the top of our model, leadership sets the framework around execution. There are three main elements that leadership is responsible for:

→ direction — through vision and leadership, management dictates the direction that the organisation will head

→ delegation — leadership is responsible for delegating responsibility and assigning accountability (plus managing the resources involved)

→ decisions — a key component of leadership's contribution to execution is the delivery of decision making.

Underneath leadership, there are two elements involved in 'getting things done': core processes and initiatives.

> Core processes are any processes that constitute 'business as usual' for your organisation and there's no shortage of examples for your business.

2. Core processes

Core processes are any processes that constitute 'business as usual' for your organisation and there's no shortage of examples for your business. For instance, at PwC, recruitment is considered key because it's a process we repeat every year and it has a significant impact on almost every aspect of the business, so it's something we try very hard to perform efficiently and effectively. Your business, on the other hand, might classify pricing, delivery, marketing, billings and collections or any other number of processes as core processes because these are processes you perform all the time and that are vital to your success. There are several elements to any core process, which I call the five 'Ds':

→ Design — the design of your core processes needs to be efficient and effective. Any process that you need to perform regularly that's badly designed is set up for failure from the start.

→ Deliver — does what you actually deliver correlate with your initial design?

→ Deploy — how do you allocate resources so your core processes can be carried out?

→ Data — any data that's necessary for managing your core processes must be adequately reported.

→ Delta — once you have the appropriate data, the next step is to determine what changes you hope to make in response to the data. This is the delta, shorthand for change.

Because you are carrying out these core processes regularly, it's imperative you do them well. However, this doesn't mean you have to get every process of the business right. Often, there are many systems within any one business that could be considered sub-optimal, but as long as these processes are not core processes, the impact on your organisation should be minimal. Before you tie yourself in knots redesigning every procedure within your company in a bid for greater effectiveness, remember that you don't have to perform every process well — just the most important or core processes.

3. Initiatives
The second half of 'getting things done' involves coming up with initiatives or new ways to improve your business's operations. Initiatives are inherently more complex to implement than core processes because they necessarily involve change and, as we all know, humans are often resistant to change.

The relationship between initiatives and core processes is symbiotic: any plans for the future of your business should feed your core processes. For instance, it could be that any merger and acquisition (M&A) activity sits firmly within the realm of initiative until you purchase the desired business, when the operation suddenly transitions to become part of your core processes.

Let's run through the elements of the initiative process.

→ Assess — first, you should comprehensively examine the process that is currently in place.

→ Design — here, your organisation can design what the future might look like by asking: 'Ideally, what would we like our operations to look like?' This design stage feeds directly into your core processes.

→ Benefits — it is crucial that you work out what the benefits of any change are. Ask yourself: I'm going from A to B — why? There's got to be a 'why' (and a fairly substantial one if the change process is going to be arduous) otherwise there's no point to your initiative and it will be near impossible to convince stakeholders to jump on board.

→ Transition — there has to be a transition stage to any initiative. It's all too common never to get from A to B because C popped up unexpectedly in the middle, so be sure to factor in a transition or adjustment period.

→ Project and change management — just as you need a transition phase, it's imperative that you have a project and change plan for any initiative you plan to implement. This plan should consist of two components. First, list all the stages you need to complete as well as all the stakeholders you need to consult, because the 'program' part of any initiative involves recognising which people you need to involve. The next (and far more difficult) step is the 'change' part: How do I get all stakeholders to agree?

→ Resource — it almost goes without saying that you need to ensure you have sufficient resources in place to carry out your initiative.

→ Accountability — you should ensure there are people who are designated to be accountable for each stage of the change process.

→ Feedback — seeking feedback will help keep performance on track.

> Initiatives are a hugely significant component of any business's operations and without change your business will become stale and stagnant, fast.

Before we leave initiatives and move on to the next element of execution, I'd like to leave you with one salient point. Initiatives are a hugely significant component of any business's operations and without change your business will become stale and stagnant, fast. However, while implementing initiatives well is important, it is not enough to ensure the sustained success of your business. Many people get very caught up in change management, often to the detriment of their core processes. Both elements (initiatives and core processes) are equally important, so don't ever neglect one for the other because you can destroy a lot of value in doing so. In short, implementing initiatives well is necessary but not sufficient to replace the delivery of value through execution.

4. Culture
The final element in our framework for operating choices is culture. Culture is

an executive tool used to manage operations and involves simply knowing the rules of the game. In poker, for instance, there is a host of universal rules, such as 'never talk at the table' and 'a fast game's a good game'. In business, culture is like the internal rules your business is playing by. The culture of your organisation governs:

→ Speed — how fast things happen. This is like your organisation's metabolism.

→ Trusts and ethics — this concept raises two issues. Firstly, how reliable is someone's word within your organisation? And secondly, is their view of the right thing to do (i.e. values) shared by others?

→ Action orientation — does your organisation value action or avoiding mistakes?

→ Focus — this is a choice you have regarding the *raison d'être* of your organisation. For instance, your focus might be customers, production or technology.

→ Incentives — what gets rewarded (both financially and psychologically) often drives the culture of an organisation.

These cultural elements generally provide a calibration of what might be feasible actions in your organisation.

Alignment

As we talked about in the previous chapter, alignment is imperative when making operational choices. For example, if you've got a high-speed culture with a high level of trust invested in your employees and you design a new process that discourages trust, then your initiative is hardly likely to win you any fans internally. Or if you have a leadership style that aims to offer delegation but your core processes are particularly rigid, then that directly undermines your leadership direction. Similarly, the very best idea will still fail if the cultural dimensions of your organisation don't suit the way the initiative has been designed, or if your leadership subtly undermines it by giving directions about other priorities.

Each element of your operating choices, each piece of the puzzle, needs to be synchronised with the others rather than operate in isolation. Failure to do so is one of the main reasons businesses fail. At this point, it's worth considering which aspects of your own culture get this wrong. Where can you see misalignment between the leadership, core processes, initiatives and culture in your company? Is there room for improvement in which core processes are performed or which initiatives are introduced? What are the barriers to these improvements?

Of course, as Russian novelist Leo Tolstoy wrote in the opening line of *Anna Karenina*, 'Happy families are all alike; every unhappy family is unhappy in its own way'. Businesses are much the same. Happy or successful businesses are all alike in that they execute all these elements of operation correctly, whereas every unhappy business can fail in its own way. Business failure might be due to the failure of a core process, or failure to implement a needed initiative. It might be that there is failure at a leadership level or a cultural mismatch of some description. There are a million ways that the operational aspect of your business could go wrong but there really is only one way to get it right — and that's through alignment.

But this is far from easy, I appreciate. It can often be very difficult to identify which element is out of sync with the others, let alone to fix it. Also, sometimes it's simply impossible to achieve perfect alignment between all four elements of business operation. But this why management is such a complex art. Moreover, just because it's complex is not to say you shouldn't try.

Calibrate

Just like a set of tyres, the other potential cause of a breakdown in operations (aside from alignment) is balance. Time and time again I see businesses that focus on only one or two elements in the execution process, say accountability and feedback, to the extent that they forget what it was they initially set out to achieve. While accountability and feedback are important, if you're perfecting the process to a degree that you lose sight of why you're actually doing it, is it possible you're over-engineering the process? When it comes to the data aspects of your core processes, it's easy to get distracted with excessively measuring something that's simple to gauge but might only give you limited insight. An example is measuring your sales process. While it's not hard to calculate the number of sales calls an employee makes, it's far more difficult to measure the quality of those calls. Yet which should you care about more? Are you, perhaps, measuring quantity over quality? Or focusing on what's easiest or most readily available to measure instead of what's most useful? It's important to keep a sense of perspective when deciding what and how to measure within your business.

Similarly, it's important to retain perspective about what it is you're trying to achieve. A leadership-oriented person will often have a tendency to focus too much on the leadership aspects of the business, perhaps even to the detriment of the core processes, initiatives and culture and how these work within the context of your organisation. Someone from human resources might want to focus too exclusively on culture, or an engineer may be preoccupied with core processes, or a consultant with initiatives and change processes. It's useful to remember that different orientations within the operational framework tend to have different emphases.

It's important to retain perspective and balance when managing the various aspects of the operation of your business and to calibrate in terms of your outcomes. For the leader focused on value, you can't afford to let any one of the elements of the execution framework have primacy.

KEY TAKEAWAYS

→ There are four elements to executing strategy in your business: leadership, core processes, initiatives and culture.

→ There is no one right answer when it comes to operational choices. But, as there are many components to effective execution, prioritisation is a must.

→ You don't have to perform every process well, just the core processes.

→ Implementing initiatives well is necessary, but it's not enough to ensure the sustained success of your business.

→ Alignment is imperative when making operational choices. Each element needs to be synchronised rather than operate in isolation.

→ It's important to retain perspective and balance when managing the various aspects of the operation of your business and to calibrate in terms of your outcomes.

FURTHER READING

Max DuPree, *Leadership Is An Art*, Dell Publishing, New York, 1990.

John Heider, *The Tao of Leadership: Lao Tzu's Tao Te Ching Adapted for a New Age*, Humanics Publishing Group, Atlanta, 2005.

PMI Melbourne Australia Chapter, *A Guide to the Project Management Body of Knowledge (PMBOK Guide) (4th Edition)*, Melbourne, 2008.

Chapter 15

Financing choices

*A banker is a man who lends you an umbrella
when the sun is shining, but who wants the
umbrella back the moment it starts raining.*
— Ralph Waldo Emerson, essayist, poet and philosopher

In 2011 the FBI arrested several men on multibillion-dollar gambling, bank fraud and money laundering charges.[55] Their common vice? Poker. As part of their ongoing investigation into poker websites in the USA, where online gambling is effectively illegal, the FBI uncovered wire transfers to the tune of US$3.6 million (£2.2 million) made to a bank branch in London's exclusive Knightsbridge district.[56]

This, however, was only the beginning.

Further investigation into online gaming sites PokerStars and Full Tilt Poker revealed that the card-playing consortiums purportedly had links to bank accounts across a full deck of countries worldwide, from Canada to Malta and from Switzerland to Ireland.

Such audacious activity flips on its head the question of how to raise your table stakes. A question, nonetheless, that mirrors the topic of this chapter: how to finance your business.

In business, just as in poker, players must consider the most effective way of raising the money needed to get into the game. And once there, how you maintain your stake to stay seated at the table. The importance of the capital question cannot be underestimated, because there is significant value to be gained by optimising the capital structure of your business. The cost of capital is a key value driver for any business. So much so that achieving your optimal capital model means you can reduce the overall cost of capital significantly. Add to this the sensitivity of overall value to the cost of capital, and any small adjustments you make to your capital may result in sizeable improvements in value.

However, corporates face an added complexity compared to those playing Texas hold 'em: in business we're not just talking about equity (i.e. your table stakes); you can also borrow money too. So the key question you should ask when assessing your capital structure is not just 'What should I do to raise my stakes?' Rather, you should be asking, 'What should I do to raise my stakes and what sort of mix between debt and equity should I employ?'

Of course, debt markets are now far from the liquid and cheap sources of finance they once were. Moreover, recent valuation uncertainties have resulted in greater scrutiny over the way that equity markets approach value dynamics. So the underlying question of this chapter really becomes: 'What should I do to raise my stakes and what sort of mix between debt and equity should I employ now?'

Instruments of capital structure

In order to begin answering this for your own business, let's examine the instruments of capital that are available to you. First, however, it's important to remember that the main considerations when choosing capital instruments are:

→   cost
→   risk and required return
→   flexibility.

        There exists a not insignificant trade-off between the variables of cost, risk and flexibility when choosing your optimal capital structure.

To give you an idea how these considerations play out, at one end of the capital structure scale is debt you obtain from a bank. Such debt is relatively cheap but, because banks tend to be risk averse, this is also a fairly inflexible source of capital. At the other end of the spectrum, private equity finance offers a far more flexible (but much more expensive) alternative. As you can see already, there exists a not insignificant trade-off between the variables of cost, risk and flexibility when choosing your optimal capital structure. In order to negotiate this trade-off you first need to work out what business you plan to be in, which will in turn provide a picture of the risk profile of your organisation, the types of returns you can expect and your needs regarding the three considerations of costs, risk and flexibility. For instance, early on in your business maturity (which we discussed in Part I), it's likely you'll need to source your capital from outlets that offer a greater degree of flexibility and risk tolerance, such as private equity finance. Once you've done this, you're ready to choose between the various instruments of capital at your disposal, shown here.

Figure 40: The capital structure spectrum

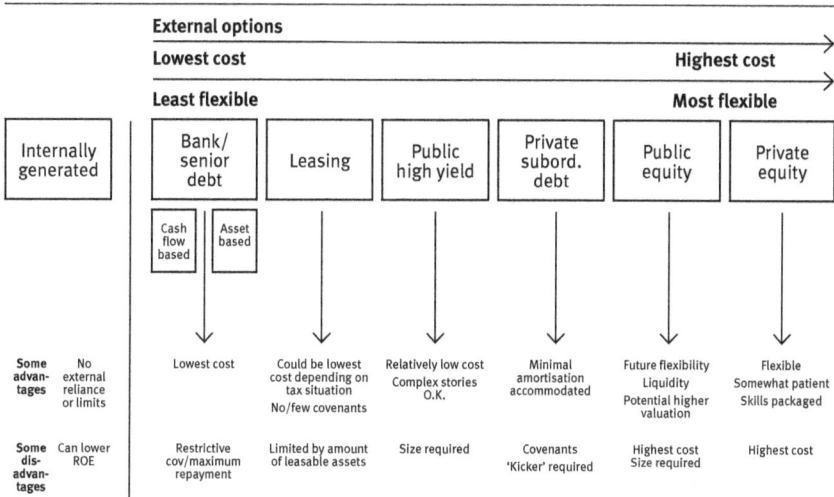

External options

Lowest cost ————————————————————————→ Highest cost

Least flexible ————————————————————————→ Most flexible

Internally generated	Bank/ senior debt	Leasing	Public high yield	Private subord. debt	Public equity	Private equity
	Cash flow based | Asset based					

Some advantages	No external reliance or limits	Lowest cost	Could be lowest cost depending on tax situation. No/few covenants	Relatively low cost. Complex stories O.K.	Minimal amortisation accommodated	Future flexibility. Liquidity. Potential higher valuation	Flexible. Somewhat patient. Skills packaged
Some disadvantages	Can lower ROE	Restrictive cov/maximum repayment	Limited by amount of leasable assets	Size required	Covenants. 'Kicker' required	Highest cost. Size required	Highest cost

Options for capital structure

Senior debt — this type of debt is available from banks or from bond holders and will be instantly recognisable to anyone who has a mortgage because it's basically the same deal. Senior debt can either be asset-backed (i.e. backed by an asset such as your house, which you can, if necessary, sell) or income related (i.e. in the same way a bank will assess your income when deciding whether you can afford a particular mortgage).

High yield — given their proximity on the capital structure spectrum, high yield debt is very similar to senior debt in all the same ways senior debt is akin to a mortgage. However, high yield debt is more like borrowing all the equity in your house on your mortgage: it's a higher risk strategy.

Fallen financial guru of the 1980s, Michael Milken, was renowned for his part in the development of high yield debt (dubbed 'junk bonds'). The principle behind it was that people went broke a lot less often than the banks priced into any debt, so high yield bonds were actually a good earn for investors. A big challenge for this sort of financing is that refinancing can be difficult when credit markets tighten.

Hybrid instruments or mezzanine debt — such capital raising is a cross between equity and debt, which offers slightly cheaper debt alongside some of the benefits of equity. It's as if I were to help you out with your home loan and offered better rates than the bank on the condition that, if the property value increases more than 10 per cent, I get a 50/50 share in that increase in value. Here, I'm awarded some equity in the property but I'm also charging you, a bit like a bond or a bank debt.

Essentially, mezzanine debt offers a hybrid style of capital raising, one that's very common in early-stage companies.

Public equity — strategies such as being listed on the share market or on the IPO (Initial Public Offering) market fall here. Public equity is a relatively expensive source of finance because people demand a return on equity once you've listed, yet it's also a fairly flexible option. Once you've raised funds for your business this way you're free to do what you want with them (within the restraints of appropriate corporate governance). On top of this, public equity is a pretty risk-tolerant choice (although some investors are more so than others).

Private equity — the most risk-tolerant option of all, private equity financiers are willing to put up with extensive risk to their funding and are very flexible about what you do with it provided you do it in consultation with them. The downside? As we've seen, there's an inverse relationship between flexibility and cost, so private equity is not cheap finance. Like most things, however, you get what you pay for.

Amount of capital

Having examined each of the capital options available to you, the next step is to ascertain exactly how much capital you need to raise. This can usually be determined by considering the following three requirements:

→ the amount of working capital you need to devote to your business
→ the amount of capital investment needed (plant, buildings and the like)
→ the amount of capital necessary for the risk you're running — risk capital, if you will.

When you carry out your business analysis (as covered in the preceding chapters and Part II in particular) it will soon become evident just how much risk you're carrying, so before you even reach this chapter you should have a good idea of the amount of capital you need, as well as why that capital is required.

> Having examined each of the capital options available to you, the next step is to ascertain exactly how much capital you need to raise.

Mix of capital

Next you need to decide on the mix of capital options for your business, or the optimal capital structure, choosing from those instruments on the capital structure spectrum and taking into consideration the costs of each instrument. In other words, what's the cheapest workable mix of debt and equity you can get away with?

In order to build your optimal capital structure model there are three things to understand:

→ How is your company valued by equity markets?
→ How might your credit be assessed by a bank or rating agency?

→ How is your weighted average cost of capital calculated across a range of leverage scenarios?

Leave off any one of these and you risk your model coming down like a house of cards. Let's look at these three elements one by one.

1. How is your company valued by equity markets?

A well-calibrated DCF model should tell you this, including the appropriate return and growth expectations of the business, and particularly its capital requirements.

2. How might your credit be assessed by a bank or rating agency?

It will come as no surprise that there exists a model to calculate the cost of credit for different levels of risk: the credit curve. The credit curve graphs the return debt providers require (factoring in the risk of the company defaulting on the loan).

> Fortunately, when it comes to corporate capital we don't need to go through all those machinations.

Think of it as a corporate mortgage of sorts. When you take out a home loan, the bank prices that mortgage by calculating what their cost of funding is. When they advance the required money to you, the interest rate incorporates a percentage charge for the possibility of defaulting (both by you and by other borrowers). Because there's some uncertainty involved in calculating this risk, the bank will also add on some extra equity capital to support that variability. (For instance, only one in 100 may be defaulters, but what if the rate is two in 100 for that particular year?) The bank then multiplies this through a formula to arrive at the interest rate you can borrow at.

Fortunately, when it comes to corporate capital we don't need to go through all those machinations. Instead, we use the relatively simple model of the credit curve, made possible by the existence of traded bonds, whose rates and degrees of credit risk you can easily find out. This can be done by using rating agencies such as Standard and Poor's (S&P) and Moody's, which rate corporates on their ability to repay debt.

Rating agencies employ a range of techniques to determine the general creditworthiness of a company, the two most common being ratios and the Merton model.

Ratios — the easiest way to predict credit costs and therefore estimate potential credit rating is to use comparative ratios such as those shown in the table below. These ratios indicate a range of risk premiums based on the perceived creditworthiness of your business. These ratios vary according to industry, but every so often rating agencies such as S&P will publish a study of the typical ratios for each grade, which allows you to see which category you fit into across the table. As an example, figure 41 shows some of the ratios for industrials.

Figure 41: Extracted key ratios by S&P (industrials) and related credit margins

	AAA	AA	A	BBB	BB	B
Debt/EBITDA	0.4	1.0	1.5	2.3	3.0	5.4
Debt margins (indicative)	50	125	175	225	400	600

The Merton model — the second tool used to calculate creditworthiness is the Merton model, which factors in volatility when predicting credit margin in order to work out the risk of default in a variety of financial leverage situations. By looking at the risk of default implied by volatility when run through an option model, it's possible to estimate the level at which loans should be priced.

> The third key issue to understand when building your optimal credit structure is how the cost of equity moves for a given level of debt.

3. How is your weighted average cost of capital calculated across a range of leverage scenarios?

The third key issue to understand when building your optimal credit structure is how the cost of equity moves for a given level of debt. There are a couple of formulas available to you: the Harris Pringle method and the Hamada method. Without going into too much detail on either, both adjust the risk factor for any given level of debt. It's worth noting that the Hamada formula allows a larger benefit for tax deductions: as you take on more debt you enjoy increased tax deductions for that debt and the Hamada formula allows more fully for this.

> Using the WACC shows the trade-off between the return the equity investor wants and the return debt providers require.

Once you understand the three key issues covered, you're ready to develop an optimal capital structure model. In order to do this, we use a weighted average cost of capital (WACC), as discussed in Chapter 3. Using the WACC shows the trade-off between the return the equity investor wants and the return debt providers require, which in turn reveals the proportion of the value of a business you may want to finance with long-term debt.

Figure 42: Optimal capital structure modelling — the optimal WACC curve

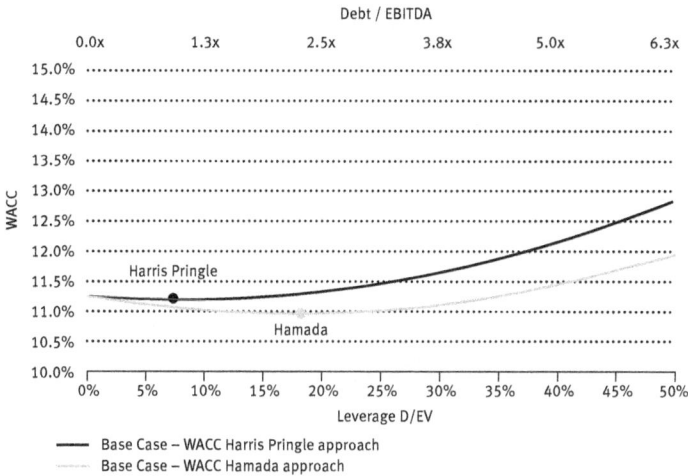

By gearing up or downwards until you reach your optimal point you can lower your overall cost of capital just by having a certain amount of debt in your capital structure. Therefore, it's valuable to think about the (long-term) optimal capital point for your business.

It is worth noting that it's possible to gear up your business in the short term. Say you want to raise your levels of private equity debt quickly and then pay that debt down over a few years; you might choose to opt for a higher level of debt in the short term. However, you'd do well to remember the refinancing risks so prevalent during the 2007 financial crisis when people borrowed at much more perilous levels than usual. Of course we all know what happened when many businesses were unable to refinance their debts as the broader economy crashed. So while it's entirely possible to gear your business up in the short term, your long-term strategy should look very different.

Capital alignment

To recap, when working out how best to finance your business you need to determine two things:

→   How much money do I need?

→   What mix of capital instruments will raise those funds?

→   (Or to put it another way, what's the optimal capital structure for my business?)

Only then are you equipped to implement strategies that will move you towards this optimal mix.

However, just because you answer these two questions in tandem doesn't mean there won't be mismatches between how much debt you should have and how much debt you actually have. This is where capital alignment comes in.

For instance, if you find you have too much debt, then it's valuable to go back to those instruments or sources of capital we covered to work out how you can raise a different sort of capital. Namely, one with more flexibility (and, in reality, more cost). During the GFC there was much capital raising going on, which raised a huge amount of equity. Yet more often than not business during this period raised capital on a big discount to the prevailing share price, and that's effectively the cost involved in raising capital. Always be aware that when you urgently need to raise significant funds, lenders or investors will charge you accordingly.

Similarly if you have too little debt (and therefore too much equity) there are options available to you to rectify this. Share buy-backs, special dividends and capital reductions are all avenues for borrowing more and then offering some of that money back to shareholders.

While these techniques are fine it's important to note there will be different share price reactions to various instruments. For example, when engaging in a share buy-back, your share price will generally rise because you're buying shares at a price in the market. Whereas if you opt for a special dividend, the price usually falls because the number of shares remains unchanged — you've simply paid out some of the value of the share that's inherent in the company, so the value of the share decreases accordingly.

Then there's the issue of your EPS (earnings per share) measures. EPS generally rise with a share buy-back and fall as a result of a special dividend. As a common indicator of a company's profitability, employees are often remunerated on an organisation's EPS, so changes to your debt/equity ratio can have a direct effect on employees' take-home pay packets, which is something to keep in mind. Also, if your company has an incentive plan requiring workers to increase EPS by a certain percentage, you'd be wise to favour a buy-back, otherwise you might increase value for the shareholder but at the same time violate some contract you have with executives or suppliers.

Dynamic capital structure

But, just as in poker where your cards change with every new hand dealt, the drivers for capital structure are not fixed. In fact, and as we saw in the GFC, these drivers can change swiftly and significantly. The successful executive will understand the riskiness of the optimal capital point in relation to the key assumptions that underpin it.

While it's necessary to carry out all the measures outlined in this chapter, these alone are not enough. You should also monitor the key drivers of your optimal structure constantly.

So what are the key drivers?

Firstly, the tax environment. Because the tax treatments of various capital instruments vary widely, the relevant tax rate will have a significant effect on the capital choices you make. For instance, interest is tax-deductible for many companies, but when it comes to profits you only receive the value of the associated franking credits when you pay out all dividends. Because most companies don't pay out 100 per cent of their dividends, there exists some loss of value there.

The main driver of the optimal capital point is, in fact, the tax deductibility of interest. However, there's a catch. Once you start gearing up too much you begin to lose some of the tax deductions you previously enjoyed because you now have more interest expenses than you have earnings to deduct them against. Again this leads to a loss of value.

As you can see it's a balancing act between achieving your optimal capital structure and maximising your tax deductibility. Still, more often than not, decisions regarding the mix of funding are based on achieving the best tax outcome available so that shareholders are in a better position. For this reason government tax changes can alter your optimal capital structure by quite a way.

The second lever of capital structure is the growth inherent in your cash flow estimates in your valuation. The higher the growth factored into your valuation, the lower your current debt capability — but this will change as your business matures, meaning you'll need to update it regularly.

Finally, because prices are dynamic, the credit curve and equity risk premium — and with it your optimal capital point — change daily. The way risk is priced on both debt and equity markets is susceptible to people's perceptions of the broader economy on any given day. So your expectations about future changes to these risk parameters are just as important as the current position. This is not a 'set and forget' type of problem. You can't, for instance, conclude that your optimal capital structure will be 30 per cent debt ad infinitum, because this optimum point will change from period to period. Failing to realise this means you can easily get out of WACC (in more ways than one).

Modigliani and Miller

A final note before we wrap up the question of how to raise your table stakes. Many readers will be familiar with finance boffins Franco Modigliani and Merton Miller, whose eponymous theorem stated that it's irrelevant how a business raises its capital. Also dubbed 'the capital structure irrelevance principle', Modigliani and Miller's hypothesis forms the basis for modern thinking on capital structure.[57]

However, on further reflection, Modigliani and Miller decided capital structure does matter because taxes matter. (In fact, as we've seen, taxes matter a lot when it comes to capital structure.) So too does the fact that you can't always borrow money at high-risk levels. Essentially, the two factors that matter most to the credit curve, and therefore to financing choices, led Modigliani and Miller to modify their hypothesis, and the capital structure we've discussed throughout this chapter is the end product of that evolution.

KEY TAKEAWAYS

→ The key question for assessing capital structure is: How much do I need and what sort of mix between debt and equity should I employ?

→ There exists a trade-off between the variables of cost, risk and flexibility when choosing your optimal capital structure.

→ Using an optimal capital structure model to determine your optimal capital point, you can lower the overall cost of capital just by achieving a certain amount of debt in your capital structure.

→ Prices are dynamic so the optimal capital structure changes daily. This is not a 'set and forget' type of problem.

FURTHER READING

Christian Bluhm, Ludger Overbeck and Christop Wagner, *An Introduction to Credit Risk Modelling*, Chapman & Hall, Boca Raton, 2002.

Tim Ogier, John Rugman and Lucinda Spicer, *The Real Cost of Capital*, Pearson Education, London, 2004.

Chapter 16

Communicating value

Communication works for those who work at it.
— John Enoch Powell, British politician

You can put your poker face away. A study has been undertaken by several prominent US academics, including a psychologist, an economist, a biologist and a brain and cognitive scientist, to examine the effects of opponents' faces on human betting behaviour. The result? A neutral facial expression may not be the best 'poker face'; rather 'a face that contains emotional correlates of trustworthiness' is preferred.[58] The study reports that a face conveying positive emotions affects opponents' decision making far more effectively than a neutral or threatening face. Moreover, opponents facing a smile were much more likely to react in the desired way.[59] In other words, break out your joker's grin if you really want to win.

The very concept of a poker face — the idea that you can affect others' behaviour just by conveying selected information — is a good analogy for just how powerful effective corporate communication can be.

Consider this: when play starts at the poker table, you can't see the other players' cards, so suddenly any information they convey, even inadvertently, is key to your game. Every word, every gesture, every movement becomes an act of communication. Has your opponent bet high? Do they slump in their chair? Are they talking up their hand? Or playing down their chances? All of these clues offer information; indeed, they are your only way of knowing anything about your competitors' hands.

Interestingly, this is how your investors feel about you.

Because your investors aren't privy to the internal boardroom discussions of your business, because they are reliant on whatever information you choose to provide (within legal requirements, of course), they are dependent on your communication with them to assess the value of your company. Here, as is so often the case in poker, you want your communications to convey to your investors that you have a strong hand.

Trustworthy communication

The poker face study doesn't just remind us about the importance of communication; it also highlights the importance of trustworthiness in communication. This idea of credibility is as central to corporate communications as it is to playing poker, and for all the same reasons. The only difference is that uncertainty is your friend when trying to bluff your opponents at the card table, whereas in business your aim is to convince investors that you're relatively risk-free. So if simply wearing a 'trustworthy' expression can award credibility to a card shark, imagine what truly trustworthy communications can add to your company.

Communication is central to managing value because it helps you to set expectations and then confirm that you've delivered on those expectations. Given that value is all about the future, expectations are vitally important, and if investors don't have their expectations correctly set then it's unlikely your company will be correctly valued in their assessment. If communication is to be of any use in creating and managing value, then it should always be devised with your investors' expectations front of mind.

Having said that, it's the way you have delivered against expectations in the past that sets the level of credibility with which people will view your communications about the future. This comes back to the need for certainty or trustworthiness in your investors' minds.

In many smaller companies, the role of investor relations (IR), or communicating with your stakeholders, often falls to the CFO or the CEO. While this may be carried out in conjunction with an IR professional, the job of communication is just one of many for today's manager, who may not have time to appreciate the nuances of the field.

In order to provide a fast but effective guide to investor relations, this chapter runs through the mechanics of communication in the form of a communication cycle. This cycle comprises four stages, each of which we'll explore in detail.

These stages are:
i) developing the message you wish to send
ii) targeting the appropriate audience for your message
iii) thinking about the way in which you deliver the message
iv) receiving feedback in response to your message.

Before looking at those stages, however, let's consider the value of communication to your company.

Benefit proposition of communication

The field of investor relations is a relatively new one and amalgamates finance, communication, marketing and securities law compliance.[60] Companies now not only communicate information regarding their financial strategies but also the broader strategic direction of the corporation and, increasingly, their intangible values too (such as the firm's policy on corporate governance or corporate social responsibility).[61]

The benefits of such communication cannot be underestimated. In their article 'Investor Relations, Liquidity and Stock Prices', authors Michael Brennan and Claudia Tamarowski demonstrate the importance of a company's IR functions for its stock price.[62] They do this by proving a clear chain of causation between:

i) corporate IR activities and the number of stock analysts who follow the firm

ii) the number of analysts who follow the firm and the liquidity of trading in the firm's shares

iii) the liquidity of the firm's shares and its required rate of return, or cost of capital.[63]

Brennan and Tamarowski conclude that 'a firm can reduce its cost of capital and increase its stock price through more effective investor relations activities, which reduce the cost of information to the market and to investment analysts in particular'.[64]

Authors Brian Bushee and Gregory Miller go one step further in their paper 'Investor Relations, Firm Visibility, and Investor Following', concluding that you can actually improve value — and in just one year — by initiating IR in your company.[65] Bushee and Miller conducted empirical tests on a sample of 210 small and mid-tier companies that boosted their IR activities and discovered increases in disclosure, media coverage, analyst following, institutional investor ownership, visibility to a new type of investor and, most significantly, value.[66]

It appears that there's quite a big bang to be had for your investor relations buck. When managed well, investor relations can improve liquidity in your stock price, which generally reduces any disparity between what buyers and sellers think of your business and what the reality is, so there's less confusion in the marketplace. Over time, improvements here can reduce the actual cost of capital for your business (mainly through the action of that improved liquidity but also through the reduction of risk). Accordingly, investor relations can significantly improve the value of your company.

The communication cycle

Having established that the benefits of effective investor relations are many, what exactly does such communication involve? The following figure sets out the key activities across the communication cycle.

Figure 43: The communication cycle

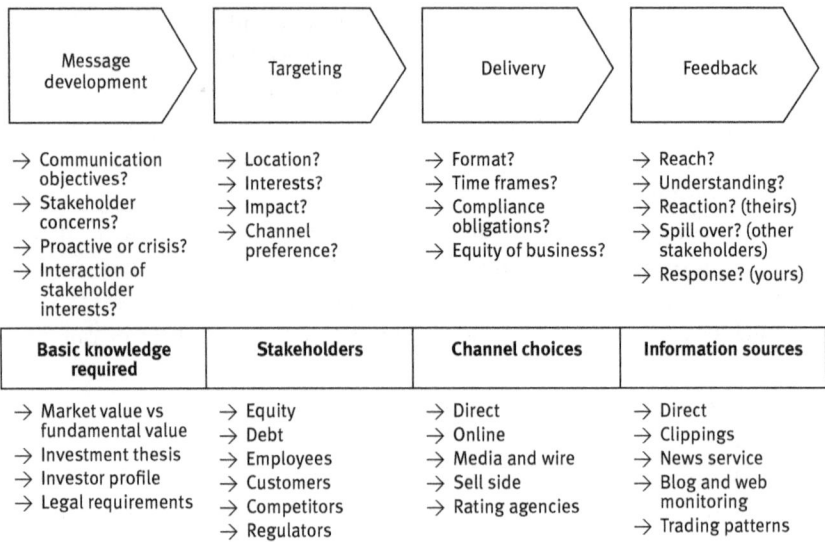

Message development	Targeting	Delivery	Feedback
→ Communication objectives? → Stakeholder concerns? → Proactive or crisis? → Interaction of stakeholder interests?	→ Location? → Interests? → Impact? → Channel preference?	→ Format? → Time frames? → Compliance obligations? → Equity of business?	→ Reach? → Understanding? → Reaction? (theirs) → Spill over? (other stakeholders) → Response? (yours)
Basic knowledge required	**Stakeholders**	**Channel choices**	**Information sources**
→ Market value vs fundamental value → Investment thesis → Investor profile → Legal requirements	→ Equity → Debt → Employees → Customers → Competitors → Regulators	→ Direct → Online → Media and wire → Sell side → Rating agencies	→ Direct → Clippings → News service → Blog and web monitoring → Trading patterns

Let's step through the cycle in detail.

Message development

Developing the message you wish to send to investors is not only the first step in the communications process, but also the most crucial. This message needs to be clear, concise and constructed with your investors firmly in mind. It should also be informed by the themes covered so far in this book — in particular, the issues of risks to value and real value adding. In order to develop an effective message to investors, there are several considerations to take into account.

First, it's important to understand any discrepancy between what your business is currently trading at and what it might be worth. Is there a gap between your view and the market's view? (That is, market value versus fundamental value?) And if so, why?

After that, consider what it is your investors really want so that you fully understand and appreciate the needs of your customers.

Next, it's imperative you understand why investors might back you. Think about what key messages your investors would most like to receive and then assess whether your company is capable of living up to this ideal. (This is known as the investment thesis.)

Last but not least, ensure you comply with all necessary legal requirements and investing regulations. Investor relations attract a host of disclosure standards and any breaches of the law (in terms of communicating misleading, incorrect or insufficient information) will attract significant penalties.

For instance, all companies listed on the Australian Stock Exchange (ASX) must comply with ASX listing rules on continuous disclosure and equal access to information. The ASX Listing Rule 3.1 states that: 'Once an entity is or becomes aware of any information concerning it that a reasonable person would expect to have a material effect on the price or value of the entity's securities, the entity must immediately tell ASX that information.'[67]

In addition, the ASX requires structured disclosure in the form of periodic financial reports, which can include half-year and annual reports and accounts, prospectuses, information statements and target and bidders' statements.[68]

On top of this, Australian-listed companies must also comply with the policies and procedures set by ASIC, such as ASIC's regulatory guide 62, 'Better Disclosure for Investors', which sets out 10 principles of information disclosure.

Targeting

Targeting investor communications is where things start to get complex because, to a certain extent, you can't. Target, that is. When you communicate your company's message to your equity investors, everyone else — such as competitors, regulators and potential investors — is listening. So when your communication hits the public sphere it doesn't just shape the behaviour and opinions of your investors, it affects a raft of others as well.

Moreover, even if it were possible to restrict your messages to a specific and limited audience, legally that's often not allowed. Nowhere is this more obvious than in the banking sector in Australia. Recent changes to local finance laws saw a crackdown on price collusion between the major banks in an effort to boost competition. Now, when one of the 'big four' banks communicates with their equity investors about their position in the market or their strategy for the future, they are closely monitored by industry regulators for any indications of price signalling. So you should exercise great care when selecting your forums of communication, in order to manage those legal requirements.

You are free, however, to consider who is most likely to set or influence price and then skew your communications to that channel. For example, if you're trying to target your international investors first and foremost, an overseas road show (which can be simultaneously released in Australia to address local investors too) might be preferable, rather than communicating with investors closer to home first.

Delivery

At the start of this chapter we looked at the importance of trustworthiness to effective communication. It's not just your messages that require credibility, but also the way you deliver them. Investors demand a convenient mode of delivery that's customised to your message and to their needs.

Unsurprisingly, there's been a significant shift in recent years towards the multimedia delivery of investor relations information. The demand for interactive data and the management of IR information through data-streaming solutions such as XBRL means that e-disclosure is now commonplace. The difficulty here lies in the fact that different regions have different reporting requirements. For example, there are rules about the type of information you can disseminate into the USA, so investor relations websites often require users to select which region they are accessing information from and then tailor any IR information to that specific geographic location. Because the internet is boundary-less but reporting requirements and investor legislation are determined along national lines, there are significant regulatory issues for you to consider here.

The bottom line is that when delivering any IR message, you should try to find the very best way to propagate it. For instance, will an advertisement in a major newspaper achieve the cut-through you're after? Or is a more targeted direct mail (DM) to investors appropriate? Maybe the aforementioned road show is the go? Or XBRL disclosure?

Feedback

The final consideration in the communication cycle is where you receive your feedback from. Since its relatively recent advent, feedback from investors in the form of investment blogs is taking on an increasingly coveted position in IR. Investors now have the ability to tell you — and the rest of the world — exactly what they think of your company at any given time. While it's important to be discerning when receiving feedback, at the very least this latest development in IR gives you a sense of whether your message has been a) delivered and b) understood. It can also prove invaluable for informing new and improved messages. Use feedback from investors and employees as a source of intelligence and as a regular means for checking how your organisation's performance and strategy is being received.

Managing crises

The final (and perhaps most important) word on communication is that investor relations is not just about good news, but also bad news delivered well. Or effective crisis management.

As I write this, Rupert Murdoch, at the helm of media conglomerate News Limited, is facing one of the greatest crises of his long career over allegations that his British newspaper, *News of the World*, was involved in phone-hacking practices. The fallout from this scandal is already immense. Not in the least on the bottom line, as *The Sydney Morning Herald* reported: 'News Corp's widely traded Class A shares fell 69 cents, or 4.4 per cent, to $14.96 in early afternoon trading on Monday [18 July 2011]. The shares are down 15.5 per cent since the end of June, compared with just 1.7 per cent for the S&P 500 index'.[69]

News Corp should, in theory, be as good as anyone at managing their public messaging. They're in the business of news, after all. So it's valuable to look at how Rupert, his son James Murdoch, and the broader News Corp conglomerate are communicating during this crisis. For starters, they walked away from their pursuit of the satellite-TV company BSkyB on the grounds that any acquisition may have appeared politically unsavoury. Next they ran some very public apologies in their tabloid press, plus some (well-publicised) personal apologies to those individuals involved. At the London select committee enquiry that both Rupert and James were required to attend, a fast-acting PR strategy aimed at maximising favourable media coverage was evident. So the Murdochs' attempts to manage the crisis, and to allay investor concerns, have centred on communicating through the media. Hardly surprising for a media corporation.

What is interesting, however, is the way that News Limited is very rapidly, and some would argue very effectively, running through the communication cycle outlined in this chapter. Of course, the jury will remain out until the issue is resolved, but by carefully (yet quickly) addressing each element in the communication chain — message development, targeting, delivery and feedback — the Murdochs have come up with a clear strategy of crisis management. This shows the importance of being able to think through this cycle at speed.

The cycle must necessarily work for any day-to-day, long-term communications from your company, such as your annual report, any results briefings and any strategy announcements; your 'business as usual' information announcements, if you will. The same communication cycle also has to work for managing a crisis.

As well as being slick with your crisis management communication you also need to reach a different audience. Almost always in a crisis situation your organisation will need to address its stakeholders directly. While many of your everyday finance messages are directed at the channels you know your investors will see or read, when managing a crisis you will often opt to talk to other stakeholders — such as customers or the general public — so you should tailor your message and delivery accordingly.

KEY TAKEAWAYS
→ The idea of trustworthiness is central to effective communication.
→ Empirical evidence shows that investor relations, when managed well, can significantly improve the value of your company.
→ When communicating your company's message to your equity investors, everyone — including competitors, regulators and potential investors — is listening.
→ Investors demand a convenient mode of delivery that's customised to your message and to their needs, so always look for the very best way to propagate your messages.
→ Investor relations is not just about good news but also bad news delivered well.

$\rightarrow$ The communication cycle should be applied to both 'business as usual' and crisis communications; you just need to be flexible in how you deploy it.

FURTHER READING

Michael J. Brennan and Claudia Tamarowski, 'Investor Relations, Liquidity and Stock Prices', *Journal of Applied Corporate Finance*, vol. 12, issue 4, pp. 26–27, Winter 2000 (first published online 2005).

Brian J. Bushee and Gregory S. Miller, 'Investor Relations, Firm Visibility, and Investor Following' (published paper), Wharton Business School, Philadephia, 2007.

Anne Guimard, *Investor Relations: Principles and International Best Practices of Financial Communications*, Palgrave Macmillan, New York, 2008.

Jeffrey Corbin, *Investor Relations: The Art of Communicating Value*, Aspatore Books, Boston, 2004.

Chad Jacobs and Thomas Ryan, *Using Investor Relations to Maximise Equity Valuation*, Wiley & Sons, Hoboken, 2004.

Key takeaways

Right now we face an era of volatility and risk never before seen in financial markets. Uncertainty is up, confidence is down and value, of course, is not fixed. Add to this the extensive changes that have occurred in accounting standards and suddenly it seems that business today revolves around value. So if you take nothing else from this book, hopefully you'll see that there's never been a greater need to understand value and to be able to assess value regardless of your role within any organisation. As the 'Oracle of Omaha', Warren Buffett, said: 'Investment students need only two well-taught courses: How to Value a Business and How to Think About Market Prices.' In today's post-GFC economy, valuation is not so much an accounting add-on as a core business skill.

It's no longer good enough to think of value as a certainty. The world is so interconnected, and information flow so accelerated, that expectations of the future change minute by minute — or even second by second in some markets. Given that value is all about expectations of the future, dynamism and variability are key when it comes to understanding value now. Value is variable and value is relative and it depends very much on the circumstances of your organisation.

When considering the circumstances of your business, it's important to recognise the risks that exist to value. Often the biggest risk is overestimating your baseline assumptions, so always opt for what's probable rather than what might be possible when carrying out a valuation. Business valuation is all about how wrong we can be, rather than how right we are.

Add to these risks the fact that both competitive positioning and prices are dynamic, and it should become obvious that assessing value is not a 'set and forget' type of problem. Competitive choices are relative, not absolute, so effective competitive choices should always take into account the other players in your industry and must never work on the assumption that your competitors' positions are fixed. Similarly, prices are dynamic, which means that the credit curve — and with it your optimal capital point — changes daily.

This book provides a reference guide to one of the biggest challenges faced by business today, namely, how do you navigate the variability of value within a volatile environment? Just as today's rooster is tomorrow's feather duster, the dynamism and relativity inherent in valuation means that by staying still in the market, you risk becoming a forgotten feather duster very quickly.

Current conditions bring not just risk but also opportunities in business valuation. When equipped with a thorough understanding of how valuations are conducted, plus ideas for assessing risks to value and tools for adding value, we all have the ability to make real changes to improve the overall competitive advantage of our businesses.

Throughout this book I've employed three very diverse analogies: sailing, gambling and poker playing. These three analogies are not just personal interests of mine but are shared by a great many Australians. Yet sailing, gambling and poker are not perfect analogies for valuation. Why? Because each of these pastimes necessarily has clear winners and losers. In a game of poker, the number of chips on the table at the beginning of the game is exactly the same at the end, except that they could well be in another player's possession. In value creation, however, if you come up with a successful value strategy for your company then you can actually increase the total number of chips on the table. A winning scenario for everyone involved, as I'm sure you'd agree (and one that more than makes up for any shortcomings in the analogies used).

Listed below is a selection of key takeaways from each chapter, effectively providing a summary of what is offered by this book. In the interests of brevity, I haven't slavishly replicated all the bullet points from each chapter summary, only the most pertinent ones. This can be read as a chapter preview or to remind you of what you've covered if you've finished reading this book.

Part I: How much is my business worth?

Sailing through Part I you learn all the valuation essentials, including how to conduct a standard valuation. The million-dollar question posed by Part I is: How do I go about setting a valuation base line? There are many considerations that must be taken into account in order to answer this successfully. These considerations are covered by Chapters 1–5.

Chapter 1	# Setting the course: price versus value

In order to be strategic about value we need to understand the fundamentals, which is what Chapter 1 offers.

→ By the end of this chapter you appreciate that price and value are not the same, as well as how to recognise the difference.

→ You also learn which circumstances of a transaction cause intrinsic value to differ substantially from the market price.

→ Finally, you discover how to shape the perceptions that influence value and, in turn, how to shift price.

Chapter 2	# Conducting a strategic and financial analysis

This chapter introduces readers to the strategic half of strategic valuation. When determining how much your business is worth, you need to conduct a strategic and a financial analysis, and readers are introduced to both here.

→ You learn how to carry out a strategic analysis using Porter's 'Five Forces' model for industry analysis and business strategy, as well as value chain analysis.

→ Next, readers are shown how to complete a financial analysis using information from within an organisation, and from its competitors.

Chapter 3	# Basic valuation, discounted cash flows and multiples

As the money chapter of Part I, Chapter 3 takes readers — step by step — through the three traditional approaches to valuation: the income method, the market method and the cost method.

→ Here, you see the importance of cross-checking between all three methods of valuation.

→ Readers learn key hints and tips for carrying out a valuation, plus I reveal some of the potential pitfalls.

Chapter 4	**Advanced techniques: residual income and real options**

Having successfully undertaken a standard valuation in Chapter 3, readers explore two advanced valuation techniques in this chapter: residual income and real options.

→ You discover how residual income works, how it's been used in practice and which companies it is particularly applicable to.

→ Readers also explore the circumstances in which real options are most valuable. Plus, how to apply real options and what the associated benefits and risks are.

Chapter 5	**Special circumstances: R&D, mining and financial services**

Again looking at exceptional circumstances, Chapter 5 examines those industries that require us to adapt the valuation techniques learned so far.

→ Readers discover how to apply the general valuation methods from Chapter 3 to the particular industries of high risk R&D, mining and financial services.

→ The techniques used in each case are different and this chapter explores how.

Part II: How do I assess risks to value?

Hold or fold? Having explored the five steps to assessing value in the previous section, Part II raises the stakes by introducing the risks inherent in valuation.

When thinking about value, this section of the book asks you consider: Where can I go wrong? Here, I outline some of the uncertainties inherent in value.

Chapter 6   How green are your assumptions?

Chapter 6 examines the first major risk in valuation: being too optimistic with your baseline assumptions.

→ Readers learn how to minimise valuation errors by examining long-term trends in key value drivers (including revenue growth, margins and capital expenditures).

→ This chapter also introduces the concept of mean reversion and how this can cause many to over- or understate value depending on the recent history of the company in question.

Chapter 7   Sensitivity analysis and insights

Sensitivity analysis is used to determine how arbitrary changes in input values will impact a particular outcome.[69] In short, sensitivity analysis is all about the 'what if?' in business.

→ In this chapter, readers learn how to conduct a sensitivity analysis, as well as why it is valuable and how it can best be used.

Chapter 8   Scenario analysis: the world through different lenses

Scenario analysis estimates the change in value, assuming specific changes in key factors. It is the process of assessing the value impact of different possible futures.

→ Here, readers understand the difference between sensitivity analysis (Chapter 7) and scenario analysis.

→ In addition, this chapter shows the value of scenario analysis and how to conduct a scenario analysis that provides meaningful information for your business.

Chapter 9   Stochastic analysis: a trip to Monaco

Stochastic analysis or Monte Carlo analysis is a method of simulation that relies on repeated random sampling. This chapter effectively builds on the previous two, because stochastic analysis combines sensitivity and scenario analyses, with the added benefit of assessing probability too.

→   In Chapter 9 you discover how to carry out a simple stochastic analysis.

→   This chapter also shows what the benefits of such analysis are and how it can be used in the valuation process.

Chapter 10   Prediction markets & risk insights

Prediction markets are innovative ways of gathering more information to help you make forecasts of the future.

→   This chapter defines exactly what a prediction market is before explaining where it can be used to improve your estimates of the future.

→   Were external prediction markets don't exist, this chapter shows how you can create internal markets or gauge market sentiment using everyday online tools.

Part III: How can I increase value?

Once equipped with a fundamental understanding of valuation from Part I, plus an appreciation of the risks to value from Part II, you stop by the poker table in order to discover how you can improve the value of your business.

If you finish reading Part III with an appreciation of the actions you can take to improve the intrinsic value of your business, then I'll have done my job.

Chapter 11   Real value adding compared to 'pump and dump'

This chapter compares real value adding with the artificial inflation of share price in order to highlight the difference between the two.

→   Here, I provide a framework for you to improve the overall competitive advantage of your company.

→   Readers learn about the elements involved in achieving real value, including decisions around participation or portfolio choices; competitive choices; operating choices; financing choices; and executing, communicating and managing your value.

Chapter 12   Portfolio choices

Chapter 12 teaches readers how to evaluate their portfolios.

→   Learn how to place bets across your portfolio to improve your chances of winning.

→   Increase value by betting where economic conditions are favourable and minimising your bets where they're not.

Chapter 13   Competitive choices

Having learned about the value-adding framework available to you in Chapter 11, you now look more closely at the dimensions of competitive strategy outlined in that framework.

→   Readers learn about the elements of competitive strategy, namely cost, offer, pricing and segments.

→   In this chapter you learn not only about defining your competitive strategy but also about refining it by ensuring alignment across the various elements involved.

→   Chapter 13 also offers an introduction to the field of game theory — a highly relevant field for assessing competitive reactions.

Chapter 14 Operating choices & execution

Again delving into the framework provided in Chapter 11, this chapter further explains the elements of delivering value.

→ When faced with operational choices, readers can use this chapter to discover how to prioritise and align the various elements of their strategy.

Chapter 15 Financing choices

Chapter 15 provides a model for optimising the ways in which you can fund your business.

→ Here, readers learn how their financing choices can change over time, as well as what the most important considerations are when deciding on their debt/equity mix.

Chapter 16 Communicating value

The final chapter of Part III, and of this book, reveals how investor relations can add real value to your business.

→ Here, I talk readers through the ways in which you can develop your cycle of communication, and about the steps to take to inform the market about each stage of that cycle.

→ This chapter also tackles the question of crisis communications and offers very real ideas for everyday business communications, plus communicating during a crisis.

Glossary

ABS: Australian Bureau of Statistics.

ACCC: Australian Competition and Consumer Commission.

ASIC: Australian Securities and Investments Commission.

ASX: Australian Stock Exchange.

Beta Factor: A measure of assessing risk based on the volatility of a security or a portfolio compared to the market as a whole. Beta is used in the capital asset pricing model (CAPM), which calculates the expected return of an asset according to its beta and expected market returns.

CAPM: Capital Asset Pricing Model. Describes the relationship between risk and expected return; used in pricing risky securities.

Carrying value: In accounting, a measure of value for an asset or company based on the company's balance sheet figures. Also known as 'book value'.

Cash Flow to Equity method: A measure of how much cash is available to pay to equity shareholders after expenses, reinvestment and debt repayment. Also known as Free Cash Flow to Equity (FCFE).

CEO: Chief Executive Officer.

CF: Cash Flow.

CFO: Chief Financial Officer.

CFROI: Cash Flow Return on Investment. A valuation model that bases a company's stock prices on cash flow, not corporate performance and earnings.

Chapter 11 bankruptcy protection: The part of the US Bankruptcy Code that describes how a company or individual can file for court protection.

COPS: Costs, Offer, Price, Segment. The elements of competitive strategy.

Core process: One activity or a cluster of activities that must be performed well to ensure a firm continues to be competitive.

Cost method of valuation: The cost or asset-based approaches to business valuation are based on the principle of substitution: no rational investor will pay more for the business assets than the cost of buying assets of similar utility.

Credit curve: The applicable margin above a reference rate for different quality debts, with the same tenor.

CRIRSCO: Committee for Mineral Reserves International Reporting Standards.

DCF: Discounted Cash Flow. A valuation method used to estimate the attractiveness of an investment opportunity. DCF analysis uses future free cash flow projections and discounts them (usually using the weighted average cost of capital) to derive a present value, used to evaluate the potential for investment. If the value arrived at through DCF analysis is higher than the current cost of the investment, the opportunity may be a good one.

Derivatives: A derivative instrument is a contract between two parties that specifies conditions under which payments, or payoffs, are to be made.

DM: Direct mail.

EBIT: Earnings before Interest and Tax.

EBITDA: Earnings before Interest, Taxes, Depreciation and Amortisation.

EPS: Earnings per Share.

FFO: Funds from Operations.

Game theory: A theory presenting strategic choices, or games, where a person's success is based upon those choices and the choices of others.

GDP: Gross Domestic Product.

GFC: Global Financial Crisis.

Goodwill: The surplus value of an entity over and above the value of its tangible assets.

Hamada method: Named after Professor Robert Hamada, a method used to help determine the levered beta.

High yield: Also known as a non-investment-grade bond, speculative-grade bond, or junk bond; a bond that is rated below investment grade.

Hybrid instruments: A security that features elements of both debt and equity.

IMF: International Monetary Fund.

Impairments: A downwards revaluation of book assets.

Income method of valuation: Determines value by multiplying the income stream generated by the subject or target company by a discount or capitalisation rate to present value.

IPO: Initial Public Offering.

IR: Investor relations.

JORC: Joint Ore Reserves Committee.

Junk bonds: *See* high yield bonds.

Law of One Price: The theory that a given security, commodity or asset will have the same price when exchange rates are taken into consideration. See the Big Mac Index popularised by the *Economist* newspaper for a demonstration of this theory.

M&A: Mergers and acquisitions.

Market method of valuation: Value estimated by examining comparable sales evidence.

Market risk premium: The difference between the expected return on a market portfolio and the risk-free rate.

Mean reversion: A theory suggesting that prices and returns eventually move back towards the mean or average.

Merton model: A model named after the financial scholar Robert C. Merton, which was developed in the 1970s and is used today to evaluate the credit risk of a corporation's debt. Also referred to as 'Asset Value Model'.

Michael Porter's 'Five Forces' model: A framework for industry analysis and business strategy development formed by Michael E. Porter of Harvard Business School in 1979.

NPAT: Net Profit after Tax.

OECD: Organisation for Economic Co-operation and Development.

Optimal capital structure: The point in varying the amount of debt and equity finance of a firm at which the availability of tax deductions and the increased cost of financial distress are balanced.

PE: Price–earnings ratio.

Post-Money: The value of a company after new financing is added to its balance sheet.

Pre-Money: The value of a company immediately prior to capital investment.

Prediction market: A collection of people speculating on a variety of events — exchange averages, election results, commodity prices, quarterly sales results or even such things as gross movie receipts.

Price: The value at which exchange takes place in a market.

Price–book ratio: Also called market-to-book ratio; a ratio used to compare a stock's market value to its book value.

Price–earnings ratio: Also called PE ratio; a valuation ratio of a company's current share price compared to its per-share earnings.

Private equity: Equity capital that is not quoted on a public exchange. Private equity consists of investors and funds that make investments directly into private companies or conduct buyouts of public companies that result in a delisting of public equity.

Public equity: Equity investment in shares of a listed public company.

Pump and Dump: A scheme that attempts to boost the price of a share through false, misleading or greatly exaggerated information. This practice is illegal in most countries.

Quality of Earnings Analysis: An analysis of earnings to determine the extent of artificial profits created by accounting anomalies such as inflation of inventory.

R&D: Research and Development.

RBA: Reserve Bank of Australia.

Real option: An alternative or choice that becomes available with a business investment opportunity. Note that this kind of option is not a derivative instrument, but an actual option (in the sense of 'choice') that a business may gain by undertaking certain endeavours.

Residual Income: The amount of profit that a company generates after deducting a cost for its own equity capital.

ROE: Return on Equity.

ROIC: Return on Invested Capital.

ROV: Real Option Valuation.

S&P: Standard & Poor's (rating agency).

Scenario analysis: The process of estimating a value, assuming specific circumstances.

Senior debt: A bond or other form of debt that takes priority over other debt securities sold by the issuer.

Sensitivity analysis: Used to determine how different values of an independent variable will impact a particular dependent variable under a given set of assumptions.

Stochastic analysis: A method of financial modelling in which one or more variables within the model are random. Also known as Monte Carlo analysis.

Value: The private worth that consumers place on a good or service in terms of its ability to satisfy their wants and needs. These private values are reconciled through a market to set a price.

Value chain analysis: A way of separating a company's business system into a series of value-generating activities.

VIX: Volatility index. The S&P/ASX 200 VIX (ASX code: XVI) is an end-of-day index that reflects the market's expected volatility based on options quoted on the Australian benchmark equity index, the S&P/ASX 200.

WACC: Weighted Average Cost of Capital. A calculation of a firm's cost of capital in which each category of capital is proportionately weighted.

XBRL: eXtensible Business Reporting Language. A standard that was developed to improve the way in which financial data is communicated, making it easier to compile and share this data.

Endnotes

1. Reserve Bank of Australia, 'Main Economic Indicators for the World Economy', 28 October 2010, from http://www.rba.gov.au/chart-pack/economic-indicators.pdf.

2. Steven Kennedy, 'Australia's response to the global financial crisis', address to the Australia Israel Leadership Forum, 2009, from http://www.treasury.gov.au/documents/1576/HTML/docshell. asp?URL=Australia_Israel_Leadership_Forum_by_Steven_Kennedy. htm.

3. Martin Wolf, 'Fixing bankrupt systems is just the beginning', *Financial Times*, 29 April 2009, from http://blogs.ft.com/economistsforum/2009/04/fixing-bankrupt-systems-is-just-the-beginning/.

4. PwC, 'Intangible assets in Australia, Future issues in challenging times', internal publication, April 2009.

5. '10-147MR ASIC focuses attention on 2010 financial reports' (media release), 5 July 2010, from http://www.asic.gov.au/asic/asic.nsf/byheadline/10-147MR+ASIC+focuses+attention+on+2010+financial+reports.
    Note: ASIC reviewed 31 December 2009 financial reports for 130 entities, comprising 70 full year reports and 60 half year reports)

6. Rebecca Urban, 'Company directors have struck gold through rise in takeovers', The Australian, 5 August 2010.

7. Michael Dwyer, 'RBA takes $3.8bn hit from dollar', *Australian Financial Review*, 28 October 2010.

8. Australian Taxation Office, 'Market valuation for tax purposes', 9 March 2012, from http://www.ato.gov.au/taxprofessionals/content. asp?doc=/content/00161737.htm&page=3#P49_2657.

9. PwC, *Valuation in Practice: What They Don't Teach in School*, presentation, August 2005.

10. William Poundstone, *Priceless: The Myth of Fair Value (and how to take advantage of it)*, Hill & Wang, New York, 2010.

11. Ibid.

12. PwC, *Issues in Business Valuation: The Practitioner's View*, presentation, September 2010.

13. Southwest Airlines, 'Liar, liar' advertisement, 1992, from http://www.southwest.com/images/ad_gallery/p_ad15.jpg.

14. Jonathan Stempel, 'Buffett says economy fell off cliff', Reuters, March 9 2009, from http://www.reuters.com/article/idUSTRE5282J820090309.

15. Usually this is estimated using the Gordon growth model, or various hold and fade models. For simplicity in this template a multiple is used.

16. Capital IQ, www.capitaliq.com.

17. Robert Fenner, 'Qantas may add long-haul routes to regain share from Emirates, Virgin Blue', Bloomberg, 7 February 2011, from http://www.bloomberg.com/news/2011-02-07/qantas-may-add-long-haul-routes-to-regain-share-from-emirates-virgin-blue.html.

18. Miller & Modigliani's October 1961 paper 'Dividend Policy, Growth and the Valuation of Shares', *Journal of Business*, vol. 34, pp. 411-413 established that firm value = PV (all future cash flow) = å [Invested capital + PV (all future EP)]. This is analogous to the situation discussed above.

19. Department of Foreign Affairs and Trade, 'About Australia: Research and Development', 22February 2011, from http://www.dfat.gov.au/facts/research_development.html.

20. Ibid.

21. Share price as of 24 March 2010 was $549 per share and overall market value was US$177.2 billion.

22. Adapted from a 2006 Stanford University lecture on valuation from www.stanford.edu/class/msande272/resources/Valuation%20Lecture%202006.pdf.

23. Eric Johnston, 'Big firm, big profit, big problem', *The Sydney Morning Herald*, February 17 2011, from http://www.smh.com.au/business/big-firm-big-profit-big-problem-20110216-1awpu.html.

24. CRIRSCO International Reporting Template — Exploration Results, Mineral Resources and Mineral Reserves.

25. Richard Stewart and Jason Boyer, 'Valuation Hot Topics: Australian Mining Interests', PwC, March 2009.

26. Usually this is regressed against ROE to adjust for differences in profitability.

27. Usually forecast growth allows a reconciliation of differences in this ratio.

28. Linda Stasi, 'Biggest Losers: the rise and fall of sin city sad sacks', *New York Post*, 13 June 2008, from http://www.nypost.com/p/entertainment/tv/item_AP3ePhdKYmPjbdQFrx0h4L;jsessionid=162C61ECCE E5C62F8D60C6A447E2B3F8

29. Ibid.

30. The law of large numbers is more formally used to characterise the central limit theorem.

31. 'The Top 100 Accountants', *Business Review Weekly*, 17–23 August 2007.

32. Ibid.

33. Stephen Penman, *Financial Statement Analysis and Security Valuation*, McGraw-Hill/Irwin, New York, 2009.

34. Ibid.

35. Ibid.

36. Ibid.

37. Ibid.

38. Interview with Andrew Denton, *Enough Rope*, ABC TV, 20 October 2008, from http://www.abc.net.au/tv/enoughrope/transcripts/s2396348.htm

39. This is known as Value at Risk.

40. Gizmag Team, 'Last minute betting plunge on Apple's tablet name: iPad shortens from 7/4 to 1/3', *Gizmag*, from 25 January 2010 http://www.gizmag.com/last-minute-betting-on-apples-tablet-name-ipad-shortens-from-74-to-13/13970.

41. Douglas W. Hubbard, *Pulse: The New Science of Harnessing Internet Buzz to Track Threats and Opportunities*, Wiley & Sons, Hoboken, 2011.

42. BBC News, 'Pentagon axes online terror bets', 29 July 2003, from http://news.bbc.co.uk/2/hi/americas/3106559.stm.

43. Charles P. Kindleberger and Robert Z. Aliber (2005), *Manias, Panics and Crashes: A History of Financial Crises* (5th edition), Wiley & Sons, Hoboken, 2005.

44. Aaron Brown, *The Poker Face of Wall Street*, Wiley & Sons, Hoboken, 2006.

45. 'How does a pump and dump scam work?', Investopedia, 3 June 2011, from http://www.investopedia.com/ask/answers/05/061205.asp

46. Ibid.

47. Google reported revenues of $8.58 billion for the quarter ending 31 March 2011, an increase of 27% compared to the first quarter of 2010; as at 6 June 2011 from http://investor.google.com/earnings/2011/Q1_google_earnings.html

48. Mr Buffett on Mr Sokol's work at NetJets, in his annual letter to shareholders, quoted in *The Wall Street Journal* online 6 June 2011 http://online.wsj.com/article/SB100014240527487037125045762331714446 69138.html

49. Ibid.

50. Jack Welch and John A. Byrne, *Jack: Straight from the gut*, Business Plus, Dublin, 2001.

51. Wikipedia entry from http://en.wikipedia.org/wiki/Jack_Welch as at 10 June 2011.

52. The Welch Way website About page at http://www.welchway.com/About-Us/Jack-Welch/Biography.aspx as at 10 June 2011.

53. A more extensive discussion of competitive alternatives is in David Besanks et al, *Economics of Strategy* (5th edition), Wiley & Sons, Hoboken, 2010.

54. As recalled in David B. Yoffie and Mary Kwak, Gucci group NV (A), case study 9-701-037, Harvard Business School Publishing, September 2000.

55. Simon Bowers, 'America's online poker fans down to their last cards', *The Observer* online, 10 July 2011 from http://www.guardian.co.uk/business/2011/jul/10/america-online-poker-fans-down-to-their-last-card?INTCMP=SRCH.

56. Ibid.

57. 'Miller Theorem' from Wikipedia at http://en.wikipedia.org/wiki/Modigliani%E2%80%93Miller_theorem as at 10 July 2011.

58. Erik J. Schlicht, Shimojo Shinsuke, Colin F. Camerer, Peter Battaglia and Ken Nakayama, 'Human Wagering Behaviour Depends on Opponents' Faces', *PLoS ONE*, vol. 5, no. 7, from e11663.doi:10.1371/journal.pone.0011663.

59. Ibid.

60. 'Investor Relations' from Wikipedia at http://en.wikipedia.org/wiki/Investor_relations as at 30 June 2011.

61. Ibid.

62. Michael J. Brennan and Claudia Tamarowski, 'Investor Relations, Liquidity and Stock Prices', *Journal of Applied Corporate Finance*, Winter 2000, Vol. 12, No. 4, pp. 26–27.

63. Ibid.

64. Ibid.

65. Brian J. Bushee and Gregory S. Miller, 'Investor Relations, Firm Visibility, and Investor Following', August 2007, from SSRN http://papers.ssrn.com/sol3/papers.cfm?abstract_id=643223.

66. Ibid.

67. ASX, http://www.asxgroup.com.au/media/PDFs/Chapter3.pdf.

68. Karen McWilliams, ACA, in conjunction with The NSW Corporate Advisory Panel, Institute of Chartered Accountants in Australia, 'Investor Relations Factsheet', www.charteredaccountants.com.au.

69. 'News Corp shares tumble on hacking fallout', *The Sydney Morning Herald* online, 21 July 2011, from http://news.smh.com.au/breaking-news-business/news-corp-shares-tumble-on-hacking-fallout-20110719-1hm4i.html

Acknowledgements

Writing a book like this while maintaining a full-time workload was quite ambitious.

What sounded easy on the New Year's resolution list wouldn't have been possible without the assistance I received from many people, for which the acknowledgement below is only a small part of the thanks I owe you.

Firstly, to my wonderful wife Ann and son, Angus, thanks for giving me the time and space to devote to this undertaking. Annie, thanks as well for your eagle-eyed review of the manuscript.

To Jan Muysken and Ash Bassili, thanks for the inspiration (in your various ways) that I should actually set out to write something like this. Thanks also to PwC Australia for allowing me the latitude to attempt *Strategic Value* and the support to get it done.

To John Studley, Mark Reading, Shane McEwen, Brad McBean, Andrew Wellington, Jason Boyer, Chris Heys, Pooja Subramanian, Lynette Nixon, Niamh Scanlon, thanks for the energy and diligence you put into reviewing various drafts of this book. You really helped me clarify issues and steered me onto the right track on various interpretations that I have offered.

Of course, whilst I have received the generous support of time and thought from all these reviewers, any remaining errors, oversights or omissions remain my responsibility.

To Claire Hutchison, my excellent PA, thanks for setting aside the time in my schedule to spend on this, as well as tirelessly scheduling all the meetings and correspondence that were required to get things organised. Thanks also to Sean Andison and David Bala for their speedy and accurate research and analysis from time to time.

To Felicity McLean and Sally Collings, thanks for the enormous assistance you both provided in terms of first drafting and researching, then editing and formatting the book for publication. It looks awesome and reads much better than would have been possible otherwise, thanks to you.

To Roz Hopkins and the HarperCollins team, thanks for your support, without which this page and all of those preceding it wouldn't have been here.

Index

About the author

Richard Stewart is a Corporate Value Advisory Partner at PwC. He specialises in corporate finance and valuation, working in the fields of strategic capital investments, mergers and acquisitions, corporate restructuring, capital raising and structuring, and major commercial transactions such as outsourcing arrangements or joint ventures. He has worked for some of PwC's most prestigious global clients across a variety of industries.

Richard writes and speaks regularly on value issues. He holds a Bachelor of Economics and a Master of Business Administration and is a Fellow of both the Institute of Chartered Accountants in Australia and the CPAs, as well as a Senior Fellow of the Financial Services Institute of Australasia (FINSIA). Richard is also an Adjunct Professor in Business Valuation at the University of Technology in Sydney.